Jonah

God's Discipline and Love

John C. Whitcomb

JOHN C. WHITCOMB

6/22/15

Whitcomb Ministries
Indianapolis, Indiana
whitcombministries.org

ISBN – 13: 978-0692310274

***

Thanks to my friends at the Institute for Creation Research, Dallas, Texas, who transcribed the audio lectures that formed the basis of this book.

CONTENTS

PREFACE

JONAH was a divinely called missionary who hated the people God told him to reach—the people of Nineveh. On the one hand, then, we could say Jonah was the *worst* missionary in all of human history, for he certainly did not epitomize God's ideal of "speaking the truth in love" (Ephesians 4:15). On the other hand, however, we could consider him the world's *greatest* missionary, for at the risk of his life he boldly preached the truth of God, and the Bible affirms that truth is greater than love (love "rejoices in the truth"; 1 Corinthians 13:6).

God's inspired, inerrant, infallible Word, even when proclaimed without genuine love, can transform people by the marvelous work of the Holy Spirit. That is why the apostle Paul could say, "Some indeed preach Christ even from envy and strife ... [but] Christ is preached; and in this I rejoice, yes, and will rejoice" (Philippians 1:15-18).

For all his faults, in the end Jonah proclaimed God's message, and God honored him. Indeed, as we shall see, the Lord Jesus elevated Jonah enormously when He said of Himself, "A greater than Jonah is here" (Matthew 12:41)!

I take this opportunity to express appreciation to Jarl Waggoner for his skill and dedication in editing this book and to our daughter-in-law, Kim Whitcomb, who spent many hours making corrections and completing the process for Whitcomb Ministries to publish it. And last, but not least, I thank my dear wife, Norma, whose prayerful encouragement, under God, has made the entire project possible.

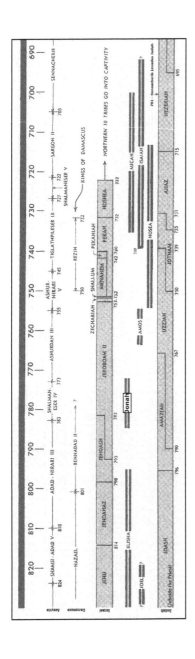

Jonah in Historical Context

(Adapted from John C. Whitcomb, "Old Testament Kings and Prophets" Chart, published by Whitcomb Ministries)

8

①

INTRODUCTION

Jonah the Prophet and Christ the Lord

AS perhaps no other book in the Bible, Jonah is a book for our day and for the tremendous challenges in our generation. As we consider the background and some introductory matters related to Jonah, we deal with some issues that are very important to our understanding of this precious, fascinating, and controversial portion of God's written and infallible revelation.

The Prophet

First, let us focus our attention on the prophet himself, Jonah. We might wonder what his parents were thinking when they named him Jonah, which means *dove*. Many times Bible characters who had wonderful names did not live up to those names. The name Zedekiah, for example, means *the righteousness of Yahweh*, yet Zedekiah turned out to be the most wicked king who ever sat on the throne of David (see 2 Chronicles 36:11-14). At least, the name given Jonah says something about what his parents perhaps were hoping, praying, and trusting God for. Maybe the desire of his parents was that he be a very soft, docile, dovelike person. If that was the case, our studies in Jonah will show that it was a false hope.

We read in 2 Kings 14:25 that Jonah came from the town of Gath Hepher in the territory of the tribe of Zebulon and not far from the Sea of Galilee. His father's name was Amittai (Jonah 1:1). Rare indeed were the prophets of God in those days, and heavy must have been their burdens as they ministered in the midst of the apostate northern kingdom of Israel. Under the leadership of Jeroboam I, the ten northern tribes had departed from the kingdom of Solomon in the time of Solomon's son Rehoboam, splitting the kingdom in 931 BC into the kingdoms of Israel (north) and Judah (south). A century and a half later, God called Jonah into a ministry in Israel during the reign of Jeroboam II (793-753).

Jonah's contemporary was Amos, the herdsman from Tekoa in Judah, who was sent up north to apostate Israel to minister God's precious Word and was repudiated for his efforts. Hosea also was prophesying in the days of Jeroboam II. In those days, Israel was prospering financially and materially, but their materialism and complacency destroyed them. In this respect, we naturally think of the United States today. What nation in the world can boast of such consistent prosperity and perhaps proportionally has less to show for it in terms of spiritual fruit?

Historical Context

In the previous century, the northern kingdom had faced near disaster. Following the apostate reign of Omri, his son Ahab became king. Ahab's Phoenician wife Jezebel brought 850 missionaries of her god, Baal, down to Israel. Had it not been for Elijah, there would have been a complete takeover, and the name of the Lord (*Yahweh*) would have vanished totally from the land (1 Kings 18).

The wicked dynasty of Omri finally was destroyed by God. Two sons followed Ahab and Jezebel to the throne. Ahaziah died after reigning only two years (1 Kings 22:51-53; 2 Kings 1), and Jehoram was killed by a mighty warrior who was jealous for his land, his people, and the name of the Lord. His name was Jehu (2 Kings 3:1-3; 9:1-26). Although we question whether he really knew the Lord personally, Jehu made a clean sweep of Baal worship, at least in its outward form (2 Kings 10:18-31).

Jehu himself, however, had to submit to the king of Assyria. In fact, his image is the only one we have of any Israelite king who ever reigned. And where do we find it? It appears on the Black Obelisk of Shalmaneser III, which shows him bowing down in homage and bringing tribute to the mighty Assyrian king (841 BC).[1] Earlier, in 853, King Ahab and all his chariots had joined with Benhadab of Damascus to stop the Assyrian advance at the great battle of Qarqar. But the Assyrians eventually asserted their control over that area, forcing Jehu and the northern kingdom to pay a heavy tribute.

Then a mysterious thing happened, and nobody knows why. The Assyrians, so mighty in that ninth century, just sort of vanished into the shadows as a mighty power, allowing the western kingdoms, including Judah and Israel, to prosper and grow and enter into a materialistic complacency they had not known since the latter days of Solomon. It is definitely possible that Assyria's eclipse in the eighth century BC was at least in part due to the preaching of Jonah. Through Jonah, God denounced the great Assyrian city of Nineveh, bludgeoning them into submission and repentance for the horrors of their wicked cruelty.

---

[1] See the picture on page 29.

Sadly, at the end of the eighth century, there came a resurgence of the Assyrians through Tiglath-Pileser III, Shalmaneser V, Sargon, and Sennacherib. The horrible cruelty and violence of that militaristic kingdom led to the final destruction of the northern kingdom in 722 BC (2 Kings 17). The prophet Hosea must have wept when he pronounced Israel's doom (Hosea 11:5). Amos also told Israel that because they had turned away from the Lord God, "He will ship you off to Assyria" (Amos 5:27, my paraphrase). They have never fully returned to this day.

An amazing passage in 2 Kings 14 sets Jonah's ministry in its historical context.

> In the fifteenth year of Amaziah the son of Joash, king of Judah, Jeroboam the son of Joash, king of Israel, became king in Samaria, and reigned forty-one years. (2 Kings 14:23)

The lengthy reign of Jeroboam II was contemporary with Uzziah's long reign at the same time down in Judah.

> And [Jeroboam II] did evil in the sight of the Lord; he did not depart from all the sins of Jeroboam the son of Nebat, who had made Israel sin. He restored the territory of Israel from the entrance of Hamath to the Sea of the

> Arabah, according to the word of the Lord God of Israel, which He had spoken through His servant Jonah the son of Amittai, the prophet who was from Gath Hepher. For the Lord saw that the affliction of Israel was very bitter; and whether bond or free, there was no helper for Israel. And the Lord did not say that He would blot out the name of Israel from under heaven; but He saved them by the hand of Jeroboam the son of Joash. (2 Kings 14:24-27)

Amazing! Here was a totally godless king whom God used to bring victory and territorial expansion to the east and north to the boundaries of the kingdom in the days of David and Solomon. How could that happen? It happened through a prophecy uttered by Jonah, who was of Gath Hepher, in the province of Zebulun and in the region of Galilee.

Here was one of those exceptions the Jews of Jesus' day had forgotten all about when they denounced Nicodemus and said, "No prophet has arisen out of Galilee" (John 7:52). Indeed, Jonah was from Galilee, and he was one of the greatest prophets who ever walked the earth. And what did Jonah do? He prophesied that God would restore the original ancient borders through Jeroboam, and that is exactly what happened.

Is it not possible that at that early stage in his career, Jonah had a glimpse of God's program for the coming kingdom age, when the nation of Israel—the chosen people, the theocracy of God—will be restored to its original power and prestige? Perhaps Jonah thought he was God's instrument to announce the coming of that great day. Yet surely he saw the godlessness and wickedness of Jeroboam II. He must have had deep concerns about the apparent contradiction between an infinitely holy God and the present godless incumbent on the throne in the northern kingdom. He must have wondered how all this fit together in light of the Abrahamic covenant promises (see Genesis 12:1-3, 7; 13:14-17; 15:1-21; 26:2-5; 28:13-15) and the Palestinian covenant of Deuteronomy 30:1-10. Could God graciously fulfill a covenant promise to His people, even when they had denied His Word and His will and abandoned His temple in Jerusalem? This must have created very serious questions in Jonah's heart.

Uniqueness

Now, let us consider Jonah in the light of the Lord Jesus Christ. Besides Moses (who was more than a prophet), Jonah is one of only four prophets in the entire Old Testament who is ever mentioned by the Lord Jesus. Elijah and Elisha, who, like Jonah, were prophets to that apostate northern kingdom in the previous century, are also mentioned (Matthew 11:14; 17:11-12; Mark 9:12-13; Luke 4:25-27). The only other prophet Jesus named was Isaiah, who came a little later and ministered in the southern kingdom of Judah (Matthew 13:14; 15:7; Mark 7:6).

The Lord Jesus mentioned Jonah several times in the New Testament (Matthew 12:39-41; 16:4, 17; Luke 11:29-30, 32), and, in fact, He chose Jonah to be His unique sign to the apostate people of His day who demanded a sign. Jesus said to them, "No sign will be given to [this evil generation] except the sign of the prophet Jonah. For as Jonah was three days and three nights in the belly of the great fish, so will the Son of Man be three days and three nights in the heart of the earth" (Matthew 12:39-40). Furthermore, in condemnation of His own nation in His day, Jesus said, "The men of Nineveh will rise up in the judgment with this generation and condemn it, for they repented at the preaching of Jonah; and indeed a greater than Jonah is here" (Luke 11:32).

Amazingly, Jonah is set forth as nothing less than a type of Christ. Jonah did not die in the belly of that great fish, as Jesus made clear. He did not say it was Jonah who was three days and three nights in the heart of the earth. Rather, He said, "For as Jonah was three days and three nights in the belly of the great fish, so will the Son of Man be three days and three nights in the heart of the earth." That is, He, Jesus, would be dead—in the place of departed spirits for three days and three nights. That is the sign of the prophet Jonah.

Jonah is unique in the negative sense that he was the only Old Testament prophet who attempted to run away from God! Why did he seek to depart from the Lord's presence? It was not because he was afraid. Indeed, Jonah was a very courageous man, for both at the beginning of the book (Jonah 1:12) and at the end (4:3), he offered to die.

Neither was Jonah offended by the thought of preaching to Gentiles. Surely, as a godly man and an orthodox, devoted Israelite, he knew the Abrahamic covenant promises. He was well aware that God had said to Abraham (Abram) in Genesis 12:3, "In you all the families of the earth shall be blessed." And that promise was repeated in Genesis 22, as Abraham, in his supreme hour of testing, offered his own son Isaac on an altar, trusting that God surely could raise him from the dead—even from burnt ashes (Hebrews 11:17-19). The boy was to be a burnt offering, yet God spared him and then repeated the promise to Abraham: "In your seed all the nations [*goyim,* Gentiles] of the earth shall be blessed, because you have obeyed My voice" (Genesis 22:18).

Yes, God is a respecter of nations. Of all the nations of the earth, He elected that one nation, Israel, descendants of Abraham, to be "a people for Himself, a special treasure above all the peoples on the face of the earth" (Deuteronomy 7:6). But God intended that nation to be His instrument to reach every nation of the world (Isaiah 43:10, 12). That is one of the amazing reasons we are here today—because He chose someone instead of no one.

That promise given to Abraham was repeated to Isaac in Genesis 26:4: "In your seed all the nations of the earth shall be blessed." The same promise was repeated to Isaac's son Jacob, as he fled to Padan Aram from a murderous brother. God met him at Bethel and said, "In you and in your seed all the families of the earth shall be blessed" (Genesis 28:14).

Over and over, through the Old Testament, God emphasized that Israel would be His channel for world blessing. It was not a strange thing for Jonah to think of Gentiles being convicted of sin and converted to God. That is, of course, how Ruth came to be an ancestress of David. God made ample provision in Israel for the care and acceptance of proselytes who would come from all the nations to hear and learn about the unique, incomparable God of Israel.

Jonah's desire to flee from God was not due to his being intimidated by the fact that Nineveh was a great and wicked city. Actually, Israel itself was a dangerous place for God's prophets as well. Ask Elijah. Queen Jezebel sought his life; and when Elijah was challenged by one army after another sent by King Ahaziah, God destroyed them with fire from heaven (2 Kings 1). The opposition and hatred of many of the northern kings and leaders against the true God of Israel was enormous. It was a risky thing to take a strong, clear, and uncompromising stand for the one true, living God.

There was syncretism everywhere, as people spoke the name of Jehovah in the same breath that they mentioned Baal. Elijah asked, "How long will you falter between two opinions? If the Lord is God, follow Him; but if Baal, follow him" (1 Kings 18:21). In much the same vein, centuries later Jesus said to the church in

Laodicea, "I could wish you were cold or hot. So then, because you are lukewarm, and neither cold nor hot, I will vomit you out of My mouth" (Revelation 3:15-16).

Israel was indeed a very dangerous place for prophets of God. Even during Jeroboam II's reign, Amos was totally rejected and threatened by the high priest of the false worship center at Bethel (Amos 7:10-17). Still, Jonah remained in Israel and prophesied there (2 Kings 14:25). So it was not the opposition he would face in Nineveh that Jonah feared but something else.

There was one thing about the great city of Nineveh that absolutely horrified Jonah. As the largest city of Assyria, it represented a nation that had wreaked indescribable atrocities upon the northern kingdom. Shalmaneser III and other Assyrian kings who ravaged and pillaged the land and tortured people would never be forgotten or forgiven. When God said to Jonah, "Arise, go to Nineveh, that great city, and cry out against it; for their wickedness has come up before Me," Jonah recoiled at the thought of making that announcement to Nineveh because he knew it was in God's character to forgive them if they repented. In an effort to forestall any repentance and humble, citywide submission before the almighty God of Israel, Jonah fled. He later acknowledged this was his reason for fleeing:

> So he prayed to the Lord, and said, "Ah, Lord, was not this what I said when I was still in my country? Therefore I fled previously to Tarshish; for I know that You are a gracious and merciful God, slow to anger and abundant in lovingkindness, One who relents from doing harm." (Jonah 4:2)

Jonah knew God was sending him to Nineveh to give the people there an opportunity to repent, for if God gave them what they deserved, they would not need a missionary to tell them they had forty days before their destruction would come.

Undoubtedly, Jonah thought God should do to them what He did to Sodom and Gomorrah; namely, destroy them with fire from heaven, with no public, official warning at all. The two angels who came to Sodom did not go up and down the streets, warning the people to repent. The people were judicially hardened, and their case was morally and spiritually hopeless; they were doomed (cf. Gen. 18:16–19:29). Jonah, however, anticipated something different in Nineveh. He believed the Lord was going to be too gracious and needed his counsel. "Don't you realize, Lord, that these people are as wicked as Sodom? Please don't send me on that mission and give them a warning. I know exactly what is going to happen. Lord, please do not spare Nineveh!" And that is the whole theme of the book of Jonah. He was not some kind of whiny, fearful prophet. He was a prophet who knew God so well that he could predict the outcome when the true message of God was faithfully and effectively proclaimed.

What an amazing book this is. In the end God has the last word. He comes across as absolutely sovereign, incomparably righteous and holy, and totally gracious. This book is filled with theology, but it is all compacted into forty-eight verses, including eight verses of poetry in chapter 2. It is a vivid narrative with superb character delineation. Even the book of Ruth, which likewise is extremely compact, is twice as long as the book of Jonah. Yet, just a few sharp, pointed words sent by the living God can drive deep into the hearts of the sinful people to whom God sends them.

May God help us to aim carefully, precisely, and faithfully in our messages, and leave God the Holy Spirit with His prerogative—namely, to bring conviction, conversion, and transformation. "Preach the word! Be ready in season and out of season" (2 Timothy 4:2), whether people like it and appreciate it or hate and despise it. There is only one thing God ever called us to do on this planet; that is to preach His Word.

Teaching

The absolute sovereignty of God on display in this book reminds us of some of the things Jonah knew from the book of Psalms. And we know he was very familiar with the psalms because he reflects their thoughts over and over again, particularly in his prayer in Jonah 2.

Psalm 115 sets forth a staggering truth the Assyrian Empire had to learn the hard way. The Gentiles taunted the Israelites, saying, "Where is their God?" (Psalm 115:2). The Israelites did not have idols or statues of deities in their temple, as other nations did. Thus, the idolatrous Gentiles questioned where Israel's God was. The answer comes back magnificently and sets Israel's God in sharp contrast to the limited, hand-carved gods of the pagans: "But our God is in heaven; He does whatever He pleases" (verse 3).

This means He has no competition or rivals. This is not a polytheistic universe. There is one God who designed it all and controls it every moment of every day. He was not at all like the so-called gods of the Assyrians or Babylonians.

Likewise, He is nothing like the modern gods of materialism, evolutionism, and naturalistic atheism. Psalm 135:5-6 says the same thing: "For I know that the Lord is great, and our Lord is above all gods. Whatever the Lord pleases He does, in heaven and in earth, in the seas and in all deep places."

Jonah would discover in his own experience that God does what He wants in the deep places. Truly, God would bring him through the most spectacular experiences any human being has ever had in the history of the world.

The book of Jonah tells us that even though people think they are independent and free, in reality they are ensnared and entangled with their own depravity and are rushing headlong to eternal disaster. The apostle Peter said:

> For the time has come for judgment to begin at the house of God; and if it begins with us first, what will be the end of those who do not obey the gospel of God? (1 Peter 4:17)

We see this in the book of Jonah, for judgment began with Jonah. If God would do what He did to get that man's attention, what would happen to Nineveh? We find the same idea in the book of Isaiah. Before Isaiah could pronounce the six woes of Isaiah 5, he pronounced the first one in chapter 6: "Woe is me, for I am undone! Because I am a man of unclean lips, and I dwell in the midst of a people of unclean lips; for my eyes have seen the King, the Lord of hosts" (v. 5). Isaiah was permanently transformed by that experience.

Until God's servants see the Lord and are purified—as Isaiah was with that coal from off the altar of the third heaven—disciplined, and bludgeoned into submission by the mighty, glorious God in heaven, we have no message at all to preach to other sinful people. We must know who God is in His infinite holiness and righteousness before we can tell people to flee from the wrath to come.

Historicity

Sadly, our generation of Christendom is on the brink of theological disaster. Many among the theological leaders in the world today reject the book of Jonah as historically and scientifically incredible, if not absurd. Even a so-called evangelical commentary on Jonah asserts that the events recorded in the book never happened. But if these things never happened, then the theology of the book is destroyed. Theology involves history—real things that God did in real times in real places with real people. That is why the Genesis Flood account does not begin with "once upon a time long, long ago." Rather, it begins in this fascinating way:

> In the six hundredth year of Noah's life, in the second month, the seventeenth day of the month, on that day all the fountains of the great deep were broken up, and the windows of heaven were opened. (Genesis 7:11)

That sounds like (and is) chronology, the backbone of history, the only context or frame of reference within which a living, true God functions on planet Earth. That is why God says, in effect, "You cannot be saved if you do not believe in My chronology."

Look at what the apostle Paul wrote:

> Christ died for our sins according to the Scriptures, and ... He was buried, and ... He rose again the third day according to the Scriptures, and ... He was seen by Cephas, then by the twelve. (1 Corinthians 15:3-5)

That means these things really happened. This is God's way of saying these are not ideas confined to some spiritual realm. No, these are real events in real history in a real world with real people.

Jesus surely knew that His precious book would be mishandled, distorted, rejected, and denied. He knew of the pious platitudes of the commentators who say, "This book is just rich with lessons and blessings, but of course these things never happened." And so, Jesus said, "A wicked and adulterous generation seeks after a sign, and no sign shall be given to it except the sign of the prophet Jonah" (Matthew 16:4). In essence, He was saying, "What Jonah actually experienced is what I am going to actually experience, for Jonah and I are similar. We are both a part of real history."

How thankful to the Lord we should be for mentioning Jonah in 2 Kings 14:25, in that very historical book filled with chronologies and genealogies and synchronisms of the kings of Israel and Judah. Let us never forget that verse when someone asks, "Did these things really happen?" May we never underestimate God and measure His power according to the absolutes of a generation that does not believe in Him.

To so many today, God could say, as Jesus did to the Sadducees, "You are mistaken, not knowing the Scriptures nor the power of God" (Matthew 22:29). Today we desperately need to know both the Scriptures and God's power if this book of Jonah is to have a message to us at all. We must know what it says, and we must know that God could—and did—really do what He said He did in this amazing and precious book.

***

Dear Father, we thank You for the book of Jonah and the amazing things You have taught us through this precious portion of Your book. May it loom large in our thinking as a message for our generation, as we face the Nineveh of our day, whether it be a foreign enemy or the Western World in all of its deepening materialistic paganism.

Dear Lord, how we thank You that You are sovereign and will not allow Your holy name to be disgraced, distorted, and denied forever. But You are also a gracious God; otherwise we would not have been saved and would not be here today. Help us to marvel at Your grace and love You for Your beloved Son, the Lord Jesus, who died on a cross and broke the bonds of death forever for those who trust Him. May these precious things fill and thrill our hearts. We ask it in Jesus' name. Amen.

Recreation of a panel on the Black Obelisk of Shalmaneser III, depicting Israel's King Jehu paying tribute to the Assyrian King. Image by Chaldean (CC-BY-SA-3.0).

The Mediterranean Sea seen from Joppa (modern-day Yaffo). Photo by Rachel Lyra Hospodar (CC Attribution 2.0 Generic)

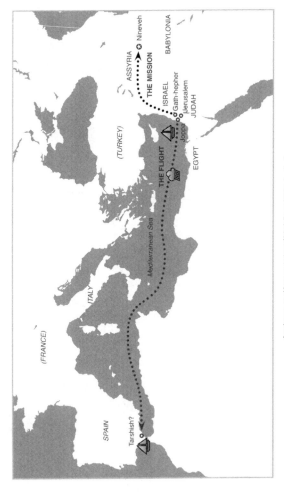

Jonah map used by permission of Mark Barry 2010, visualunit.me

②

THE SHIP AND THE STORM

Jonah 1:1-16

Now the word of the Lord came to Jonah the son of Amittai, saying, "Arise, go to Nineveh, that great city, and cry out against it; for their wickedness has come up before Me." (Jonah 1:1-2)

IN God's commissioning of Jonah, we find no explanation given and no promise of success. That is totally different from the way God dealt with Moses, when it seemed like there were hours and hours of "give and take" there at the burning bush, as the Lord overcame one objection after another (Exodus 3–4). Moses was given all the theological ammunition he could ever use, along with sign-miracles to back up his ministry.

God wonderfully prepared Isaiah also (Isaiah 6), giving the prophet a glimpse of the Lord seated upon His throne. The One Isaiah saw, we are told, was the preincarnate Christ, according to John 12:37-41. What a preparation for ministry that was, as Isaiah was cleansed, called, and told exactly what he could expect. Jeremiah also asked questions, resisted, doubted, and feared, and God patiently responded (Jeremiah 1).

All Jonah got was "arise and go." No doubt such terse instructions presuppose some ministry background and knowledge of God, as indicated in 2 Kings 14:25, where we are told Jonah already had uttered a great prophecy. Apparently he had a significant ministry prior to the command in Jonah 1:1.

Where was Nineveh? As the crow flies, it was 550 miles east of Israel. The city of Nineveh had been established after the Tower of Babel dispersion by none other than Nimrod (Genesis 10:8-11). Situated on the Tigris River east of the Euphrates, it had a history of militarism and power. It was the power center of the great Fertile Crescent, governing Babylon to the south and Syria to the west. After the time of this book, Nineveh became one of the greatest centers of military conquest in the history of the ancient world. It produced magnificent, powerful, and cruel generals, such as Tiglath-Pileser III, Shalmaneser V, Sargon, and the notorious Sennacherib, who defied the living God at the walls of Jerusalem, only to have his army destroyed by the Angel of the Lord in one night (2 Kings 19:35-36).

The northern kingdom, however, was not delivered from the Assyrian onslaught. The capital, Samaria, fell in 722 BC, and most of the population was deported to the east. Sennacharib's son Esarhaddon finished the deportation of Israelites, replacing them with other peoples. Those imported into the territory of Israel mixed with the remaining population, producing a mongrel race known as the Samaritans (2 Kings 17).

The last and greatest of the kings of Assyria was Ashurbanipal. He built a huge library and a great palace, and he beautified the Assyrian capital, which had been moved to Nineveh by Sennacherib. Assyria is listed more than once in the Old Testament as the greatest oppressor Israel faced after Egypt and before Babylon.

The Lord described the wickedness of Nineveh as coming up before Him. Everything we do, think, and say comes up before the living God, who watches, weighs, and measures every thought and motive of every heart in the entire world. Oh, how wicked Nineveh was! God later used a prophet by the name of Nahum to denounce that city:

Where is the dwelling of the lions, and the feeding place of the young lions, where the lion walked, the lioness and lion's cub, and no one made them afraid? The lion tore in pieces enough for his cubs, killed for his lionesses, filled his caves with prey, and his dens with flesh.

"Behold, I am against you," says the Lord of hosts, "I will burn your chariots in smoke, and the sword shall devour your young lions; I will cut off your prey from the earth, and the voice of your messengers shall be heard no more."

Woe to the bloody city! It is all full of lies and robbery. Its victim never departs. The noise of a whip and the noise of rattling wheels, of galloping horses, of clattering chariots! Horsemen charge with bright sword and glittering spear. There is a multitude of slain, a great number of bodies, countless corpses—they stumble over the corpses—because of the multitude of harlotries of the seductive harlot, the mistress of sorceries, who sells nations through her harlotries, and families through her sorceries. (Nahum 2:11–3:4)

Zephaniah the prophet gave the word of finality concerning Nineveh:

> This is the rejoicing city that dwelt securely, that said in her heart, "I am it, and there is none besides me." How has she become a desolation, a place for beasts to lie down! Everyone who passes by her shall hiss and shake his fist. (Zephaniah 2:15)

To cap it all, the king of Nineveh who heard Jonah's message of doom and called for repentance acknowledged the wickedness of his people and the justice of God's judgment:

> But let man and beast be covered with sackcloth, and cry mightily to God; yes, let every one turn from his evil way and from the violence that is in his hands. Who can tell if God will turn and relent, and turn away from His fierce anger, so that we may not perish? (Jonah 3:8-9)

The wickedness of Nineveh was no secret to God, and it was no secret to God's people and God's prophets either.

> *But Jonah arose to flee to Tarshish from the presence of the Lord. He went down to Joppa, and found a ship going to Tarshish; so he paid*

> *the fare, and went down into it, to*
> *go with them to Tarshish from the*
> *presence of the Lord.* **(Jonah 1:3)**

The call to go to Nineveh and "cry out against it" was a formidable assignment for one missionary—one prophet from God. In a sense, it is not surprising that we read that "Jonah arose to flee to Tarshish from the presence of the Lord." We saw the reasons he fled, and his real concern—the burden that tore him to pieces— was that God might save the Assyrians from the total destruction they deserved. He could not handle that possibility; so he fled from the presence of the Lord, 35 miles west to the sea-coast city of Joppa, in order to go 2500 miles to Tarshish (Tartessus), in what is today the land of Spain.

> Jonah is the only book in the Hebrew Scriptures devoted to God commanding a Jewish prophet to go to Gentiles and preach repentance. Nineveh was the capital of the evil Assyrian Empire.
>
> To Christians, Joppa is best known as the home of Simon the tanner, where the apostle Peter received a vision from the Lord. Peter, a Jew who kept kosher, saw a sheet lowered from heaven containing all types of non-

kosher animals. God told him, "Rise, Peter; kill and eat" (Acts 10:13). When Peter refused, God told him, "What God has cleansed you must not call common" (v. 15).

God was telling Peter the good news of salvation in Christ was not exclusively for the Jewish people; He was including the Gentiles also. The event led to Peter taking the gospel to the Gentiles via Cornelius, a Roman centurion who had been seeking the truth.

Perhaps Joppa could be considered a pivotal city in taking God's message to the Gentiles. Jonah attempted to flee from there when told to go to the Gentile Assyrian Empire, and years later the Lord commissioned Peter there to go to the Gentiles of the Roman Empire.[1]

We should not think that Jonah was trying to escape the omnipresence of God. He certainly knew Psalm 139, which gives a hypothetical case of a person imagining that he might try to run away from the Lord.

---

[1] Thomas C. Simcox, "Joppa, Down by the Sea," *Israel My Glory,* May/June, 2014, 30.

Where can I go from Your Spirit? Or
where can I flee from Your presence?

If I ascend into heaven, You are there;
if I make my bed in hell, behold, You
are there.

If I take the wings of the morning, and
dwell in the uttermost parts of the sea,
even there Your hand shall lead me,
and Your right hand shall hold me.
(Psalm 139:7-10)

Jonah knew that, of course. So what does it
mean, then, to "flee ... from the presence of the
Lord"? This is a technical expression that means
to go away from the special places God has
appointed for His servants to honor and worship
Him in spirit and in truth. That was David's
complaint against King Saul when David was
fleeing from the wrath of his royal enemy: that
Saul had driven him away from "the presence of
the Lord" (1 Samuel 26:19-20 NASB). David
ended up in Philistia. He knew God was there,
but he no longer had access to the places in
Israel where God's people worshiped the Lord.
That is the point here. Jonah did not want to be
that close to his Lord, to be accessible to His
Word and His convicting work. Jonah thought
that if only he could leave the Holy Land, God

might leave him alone, and he could somehow make a new life in a foreign land.

Of course, from our vantage point, we can easily criticize Jonah. We know that God has an answer to every situation we can possibly imagine. However, the will of God is not always pleasant to us; sometimes it can seem a very negative thing. Yet God told us three thousand years ago through Solomon:

> Trust in the Lord with all your heart, and lean not on your own understanding; in all your ways acknowledge Him, and He shall direct your paths. (Proverbs 3:5-6)

The Lord could have said to Jonah, "Jonah, just trust Me. Leave your reasonings, doubts, and fears to Me. I am very intelligent and have been here a long time. I know a great deal about people, including you. Just leave with Me your doubts, and I will make your paths straight."

The safest place to be on planet Earth is in the center of God's will. Yet some people are afraid to go to a particular mission field because something bad might happen to them there. This reminds me of John Glenn, the first of our American astronauts to safely circle the earth in space. He survived space travel but almost did not survive a fall at home, when he slipped in the bathtub. We need to leave our imaginations and fears to God. What He says and the way He directs in His providential leading in our lives must be the absolute goal for our lives. How sad it is when we abandon the will of God. But amazingly, the opportunity and the enticement to stray farther and farther from His will always seems to be present. Satan sees to that. We might wish human history were different and God would block automatically and supernaturally every effort on the part of any of His people to walk off the straight and narrow path, but that is not His plan.

God will not automatically block the way of those who flee from Him. In fact, all looked good for Jonah as he went down to Joppa. He just happened to find a ship waiting for him, and he just happened to have the money to pay, and he boarded the ship to go to Tarshish, away from the presence of the Lord.

In the Old Testament, Tarshish was proverbial for the most distant place on the face of the earth one could possibly go. In speaking of the city of Tyre, the book of Ezekiel describes for us in chapter 27 what a ship of Tarshish was like. It was the spectacular luxury liner of the ancient world.

> The ships of Tarshish were carriers of
> your merchandise. You were filled
> and very glorious in the midst of the
> seas. (Ezekiel 27:25)

What magnificent ships they were, filled with great treasures to go great distances! Solomon had ships of Tarshish that brought him apes, peacocks, and all kinds of exotic creatures, along with gold and silver to adorn his palace (1 Kings 10:22). So here was Jonah, seemingly secure, safe, and away from God, but not realizing that God had put him into His own prison and locked him in.

> *But the Lord sent out a great wind*
> *on the sea, and there was a mighty*
> *tempest on the sea, so that the ship*
> *was about to be broken up. Then*
> *the mariners were afraid; and*
> *every man cried out to his god, and*
> *threw the cargo that was in the*
> *ship into the sea, to lighten the*
> *load.* **(Jonah 1:4-5a)**

As the ship began to glide westward over the sea, and the Holy Land faded off in the distance to the east, the Lord suddenly hurled a great wind on the sea. It was such a violent storm that the ship was about to break up. "Sent out," or "hurled," is a special Hebrew verb to describe the anger of God. The storm proclaimed the omnipotence of God more eloquently than mere words ever could. Pagan sailors got the message first. They became afraid, and "every man cried out to his god."

These sailors came from Palestine, Phoenicia, Philistia, and other seaports where every god known in the ancient world was honored by somebody. They were totally gripped with terror, for they had never experienced a storm like this. All of a sudden, they became very religious.

Such a response is not unheard of even today. Consider what happened when an earthquake hit Southern California in 1994. An article from *Christianity Today* explained:

> California's $3-billion-a-year pornographic movie industry is viewing the earthquake as God's personal destruction of America's most wicked city, some porn producers say.
>
> The quake was centered in the cities of Northridge, Chatsworth, and Canoga Park, which are home to nearly all of the U.S. soft- and hard-porn video industry. Every one of the primary porn studies and distributors, a total of around 70, suffered damage. The headquarters of the largest, VCA Pictures, collapsed, destroying equip-

ment and most copies of several films. At least for the moment, high-level porn studio executives and models are edgy.

An executive at World Modeling, a San Fernando Valley agency supplying actors to the porn industry, says clients are backing away from X-rated acting as a result of the cataclysm.

"Our clients have a definite lack of motivation," says the agent for porn actors, who requested anonymity. "It's put the fear of God in them. I'm telling you, it's enough to give you an attack of religion."

"Can you imagine how the fundamentalists are going to leap on this when the smoke clears?" says a porn film director who works for many Northridge studios and asked not to be identified. "They'll say it's God's retribution."[2]

Dr. Henry Morris, with whom I had the privilege many years ago of coauthoring a book called *The Genesis Flood*, made a profound study of events like this and came to the conclusion that God's providential interventions and work-

---

[2] Perucci Ferraiuolo, "Earthquake," *Christianity Today*, March 7, 1994: 57.

ings with human beings sometimes border so closely on the miraculous that it is hard, at first glance, to tell the difference. Dr. Morris called these providential works "class B miracles." So, what, then, would be a "class A miracle"? The Bible demonstrates that when God gets into supernatural, sign-miracle judgments, it is not just one or two places that get partially damaged. Everything collapses, with special focus on wicked people. That will happen, I believe, in the coming Great Tribulation, when every mountain will be moved, and every island will be destroyed, and all the cities of the world will collapse (Revelation 16:17-21). By the time God is through with this planet, culminating at Armageddon, every single unbeliever will be removed from the world. That is a sign-miracle judgment.

The storm on the sea was not a sign-miracle but a powerful, providential work of God designed to convey a message. Through such works God is systematically, continually, and in various ways, communicating with the human race about its depravity, rebellion, and suppression of truth. He is saying this world is not here forever and man is not in charge of everything, and He is giving samples of what is coming on a cosmic and global scale. Such was the case when Jesus spoke of an incident in His day when a wall fell on eighteen people and killed them. Jesus said, "Do you think that they were worse sinners than all other men who dwelt in Jerusalem? I tell you, no; but unless you repent you will all likewise perish" (Luke 13:4-5).

To some degree, God's providential message got through to the pagan sailors. They understood immediately that their lives were in danger, and they sensed the need to call out to their gods. In addition, they began to throw the cargo overboard, hoping that lightening the ship might keep it from sinking. With their lives at stake, they did not sit around discussing what to do with their baggage.

> *But Jonah had gone down into the lowest parts of the ship, had lain down, and was fast asleep.* **(Jonah 1:5b)**

In the midst of this terrible storm, Jonah was fast asleep. I would liken this experience to that of the three disciples whom Jesus asked to pray in Gethsemane. Over and over, Jesus came and found them sound asleep, utterly exhausted from the stress and fear of what was happening (Matthew 26:36-46). Their failure to remain alert and in prayer did not mean they were resisting the Lord or that they had abandoned Him; it simply meant that in the battle their spirit was willing but their flesh was weak. Jonah too was emotionally exhausted.

> *So the captain came to him, and said to him, "What do you mean, sleeper? Arise, call on your God; perhaps your God will consider us, so that we may not perish."* **(Jonah 1:6)**

How paradoxical that the captain of the ship, a pagan, came and preached to Jonah, the prophet of the Lord. More than once in my own life, I have been rebuked by somebody who had no real knowledge of the things of the Lord but, thankfully, was an instrument God used to bring conviction in my heart.

Apparently Jonah did nothing in response to the captain's plea. He did not call for a prayer meeting or thank the captain for awakening him to pray.

> *And they said to one another, "Come, let us cast lots, that we may know for whose cause this trouble has come upon us." So they cast lots, and the lot fell on Jonah.* **(Jonah 1:7)**

The casting of lots in the Old Testament, in the pre-Pentecost era of the theocracy of Israel, was a special provision God made for His people to determine the will of God in times of crisis for the nation. The high priest had the Urim and the Thummim, which was available in the earlier years (Exodus 28:30; Numbers 27:21; 1 Samuel 28:6). We recall how Jonathan was selected by casting lots (1 Samuel 14:42). We know also that the twelfth apostle was chosen to replace Judas Iscariot by the casting of lots (Acts 1:26). That was legitimate and of the Lord. Interestingly, however, that was the last time any such method is recorded as being used with God's blessing. Shortly after that, the church age began; and through His precious Word, the completed canon of inspired Scripture, illumined by the Holy Spirit, God now provided a higher and better way to reveal His will.

We remember yet another man in the Bible upon whom the lot fell. His name was Achan. The whole army of Israel was defeated because one man, Achan, had deliberately defied the revealed will of God concerning the city of Jericho, which was devoted to destruction and under the curse of God. Conniving with his own family, he greedily took silver, a wedge of gold, and a Babylonian garment and hid them under the floor of his tent, thinking that somehow God was not aware. But, of course, as the lot focused on his tribe, clan, and family, and the crescendo of God's footsteps came closer and closer, Achan was trapped by the living God, and his deliberate disobedience was publicly revealed as that which had brought defeat to the whole army. Joshua told him to confess before God, and Achan did. He was then stoned to death, along with his whole family. A heap of stones over his body became a memorial of that rebellion (Joshua 7:1-26).

> *Then they said to him, "Please tell us! For whose cause is this trouble upon us? What is your occupation? And where do you come from? What is your country? And of what people are you?" So he said to them, "I am a Hebrew; and I fear the Lord, the God of heaven, who made the sea and the dry land."* **(Jonah 1:8-9).**

When the lot fell on Jonah, identifying him as the cause of their trouble, the sailors began to interrogate him with question after question. They were desperate and overwhelmed by the fact that the villain had been discovered.

For everything negative we could say about Jonah at this point, his response was very impressive. Jonah told his questioners that he did

48

not represent some local deity confined to a land somewhere in the Near East. He worshiped the God who created the oceans. Jonah must have believed Exodus 20:11: "For in six days the Lord made the heavens and the earth, the sea, and all that is in them." He was committed to the truth stated in Psalm 95:5: "The sea is His, for He made it; and His hands formed the dry land."

Not only that, but Jonah also said that he was a Hebrew, part of the chosen nation of this great God of creation. He belonged to God's very special people; and he was special within that nation because he feared the Lord God, unlike the many apostate Hebrews and Baal-worshipers in Israel. Putting it in our language, we would say he was born again, regenerated, justified by faith, and indwelt by the Holy Spirit.

> *Then the men were exceedingly afraid, and said to him, "Why have you done this?" For the men knew that he fled from the presence of the Lord, because he had told them.* (Jonah 1:10)

Jonah also told the sailors that he was fleeing from the immediate presence of the manifestation of the glory of the Lord in the Holy Land. This made them extremely fearful. Now they had the whole picture. Here was one of God's special people, but he was in deliberate defiance of the God who made the oceans. Surely, he had brought disaster upon them all.

There is a corporate identification in head-ship relationships in mankind that is mysterious and marvelous. One man's sin, rebellion, and disobedience brought near disaster to this entire ship, its crew, and its captain.

> *Then they said to him, "What shall we do to you that the sea may be calm for us?"—for the sea was growing more tempestuous.* **(Jonah 1:11)**

With the sea becoming increasingly stormy, the fearful sailors asked what should be done to Jonah. They were more horrified at his dis-obedience than he was, and they understood that something had to be done. But what?

> *And he said to them, "Pick me up and throw me into the sea; then the sea will become calm for you. For I know that this great tempest is because of me."* **(Jonah 1:12)**

God must have said something to Jonah that was not recorded. God must have told him that the only possible way his open disobedience to God could be dealt with righteously was for him to be thrown into the ocean. Of course, Jonah knew that had to mean death. He would die for his disobedience, for God would not allow Jonah to warp and twist the concept of God in the minds of these men in the ship. They needed to know that He was a righteous God, as well as infinite in power. Jonah accepted the fact that the great storm was his fault, and he was willing to suffer the consequences.

> *Nevertheless the men rowed hard to return to land, but they could not, for the sea continued to grow more tempestuous against them. Therefore they cried out to the Lord and said, "We pray, O Lord, please do not let us perish for this man's life, and do not charge us with innocent blood; for You, O Lord, have done as it pleased You."*
> **(Jonah 1:13-14)**

What is really surprising is that the sailors were reluctant to do what Jonah told them. Jonah had endangered their lives, and they had lost their cargo as Jonah slept; so we might think they would have been thankful to throw him overboard. But that was not their response. Instead, they continued their efforts to row to shore.

These men had a deep-seated conviction that killing a human being was a very serious matter, even in their circumstances. When the Genesis Flood ended, God said that if a man's blood is shed—that is, in cold-blooded murder—the murderer's blood is to be shed (Genesis 9:6). This is capital punishment, and it is required because the murderer has struck at the image and likeness of God. You can kill all the animals in the world, but when you touch a human being and bring him to death, you will suffer with the loss of your life. This is also New Testament truth. Paul said, "If I am an offender, or have committed anything deserving of death, I do not object to dying" (Acts 25:11).

Here, then, were pagans, godless men, showing extraordinary kindness to this Israelite. Is it not interesting that eight hundred years later another ship crossed the Mediterranean, and another storm, a Euroclydon, took hold of that ship and totally terrified all the passengers? The key man aboard was not running away from the Lord but was in His will and became a mighty hero during that trip. He told the crew and passengers of that ship:

> "I urge you to take heart, for there will
> be no loss of life among you, but only
> of the ship. For there stood by me this

> night an angel of the God to whom I
> belong and whom I serve, saying, 'Do
> not be afraid, Paul; you must be
> brought before Caesar; and indeed
> God has granted you all those who
> sail with you.' Therefore take heart,
> men, for I believe God that it will be
> just as it was told me." (Acts 27:22-25).

There were nearly three hundred men on that ship. When they landed on the island of Malta, Luke said that the natives showed extraordinary kindness to them. Pagans sometimes have a deeper sensitivity to the value of human life and appreciate God's providential workings more than God's own people do, "for the sons of this world are more shrewd in their generation than the sons of light" (Luke 16:8). Indeed, Paul wrote:

> For you see your calling, brethren,
> that not many wise according to the
> flesh, not many mighty, not many
> noble, are called. But God has chosen
> the foolish things of the world to put
> to shame the wise, and God has
> chosen the weak things of the world to
> put to shame the things which are
> mighty. (1 Corinthians 1:26-27).

Jonah was in the wrong place at the wrong time, doing the wrong thing. The only people doing the right thing were those we would think would be doing wrong. They did everything they could to save Jonah, but they realized this storm was supernaturally wrought as a result of Jonah's disobedience and eventually concluded there was nothing they could do to protect him.

The sailors pleaded with God for their lives. They understood that God had done as He had pleased and brought the storm and used the lots to pinpoint the villain. They got the message and realized it was absolutely useless to fight against the power and wisdom and purpose of the God of Jonah. In the end they fared better than Jonah, who had wished for the destruction of hundreds of thousands of Ninevites. These pagans had just risked their own lives to save his.

We find something similar in the book of Acts, where, invariably, it was the Roman centurions who turned out to be gracious, kind, and wise, especially to the apostles. God's own people—the scribes, the Pharisees, and the Sadducees—were the wicked murderers. Those Satan loves to use for his purposes are not obnoxious, loathsome, and stupid people. He loves to use brilliant people—eloquent, polished, sophisticated people—who talk religiously and have open Bibles and ecclesiastical vestments and appear to be experts in theology. Through the mouths of those who profess to be ministers of righteousness and angels of light, he can spew his venom of blasphemy. That is the disaster of our generation.

> *So they picked up Jonah and threw him into the sea, and the sea ceased from its raging. (Jonah 1:15)*

These mariners decided to obey God! They picked up Jonah and threw him into the sea, and instantly the sea stopped its raging. God had already revealed that He could do things like that.

> You who still the noise of the seas, the noise of their waves, and the tumult of the peoples. (Psalm 65:7)

> You rule the raging of the sea; when its waves rise, You still them. (Psalm 89:9)

This is God's specialty. In fact, there is a special psalm that tells us what God can do in the ocean.

> Those who go down to the sea in ships, who do business on great waters,

> They see the works of the Lord, and His wonders in the deep.

For He commands and raises the stormy wind, which lifts up the waves of the sea.

They mount up to the heavens, they go down again to the depths; their soul melts because of trouble.

They reel to and fro, and stagger like a drunken man, and are at their wits' end.

Then they cry out to the Lord in their trouble, and He brings them out of their distresses.

He calms the storm, so that its waves are still.

Then they are glad because they are quiet; so He guides them to their desired haven.

Oh, that men would give thanks to the Lord for His goodness, and for His wonderful works to the children of men!

Let them exalt Him also in the assembly of the people, and praise Him in the company of the elders. (Psalm 107:23-32)

God will never let us forget what He did on the Sea of Galilee one night when Jesus, the One who created the oceans, spoke, and instantly there was a calm. The twelve disciples fell down in terror and asked, "Who can this be, that even the wind and the sea obey Him!" (Mark 4:41).

To the sailors, the miracle at the end of the storm was greater than the beginning. The minute Jonah's body splashed into the ocean, there was a perfect calm. They really became religious then.

> *Then the men feared the Lord exceedingly, and offered a sacrifice to the Lord and took vows.* (Jonah 1:16)

The ship became a theological seminary. God had the attention of these seasoned sailors, and they "feared the Lord exceedingly." Everybody was volunteering for courses such as: "How to Approach a Holy God," or "What Kind of Sacrifices and Vows Will He accept?" or "Can We Keep on Knowing and Serving God?" This was a whole ship full of new disciples. Since the cargo had been dumped, they probably decided to head back to the Holy Land and reenter the port at Joppa. We can only wonder what happened in later years to that crew.

Sometimes what God leaves unsaid is more spectacular than what He actually tells us. He leaves it to our sanctified imaginations to fill in the blanks. I would like to offer the following suggestion for us to consider.

The last thing those men knew of Jonah was that he was dead. For them, the book of Jonah had ended right there: "And so, Jonah died." Jonah had courageously saved their lives by sacrificing his own. But as the ship glided along on that glassy sea, those sailors must have thought of how tragic it was for a man to oppose and flee from a God like this. I wonder if they got back to Joppa and in later years discovered the very strange thing that happened in Nineveh, when the city was transformed through the preaching of an evangelist who had emerged from the ocean.

The Holy Spirit tells us Jonah's story did not end out there on the sea. Even as the ship moved on, Jonah was on his way back to the Promised Land, and he had a free ticket in God's magnificent, organic submarine.

This is the point at which many readers say, "I'm sorry. That is impossible." They cannot believe that as the ship went away, under the ocean Jonah was perfectly alive inside the stomach of a gigantic fish heading straight back east to disgorge him onto the shore and launch his ministry.

There are times when the Lord puts us to the test, and here is one of them. Do you trust Him? Do you think He deliberately deceives His people? Do you think He lies? No, He is the "God, who cannot lie" (Titus 1:2).

To reject this part of Jonah's story is to reflect the same mentality that says, "A man cannot be crucified and come out of the grave three days later. It is impossible." But the Bible says that unless you believe in your heart that God raised Jesus from the dead, you cannot be saved (Romans 10:9-10). That One who rose from the dead said that His resurrection was similar to what happened to Jonah (Matthew 12:40). Jonah rose, as it were, from the dead. As far as the world was concerned, he was gone. Who could imagine being thrown into an ocean and popping up five hundred miles away three days later? I have searched for years to find an analogy to this in modern times or in historical records. I thought I had found a couple of cases of people being swallowed by large fish and surviving the ordeal, but on closer inspection, the reports proved very doubtful. This was a very special miracle. God wants us to believe Him because of who He is, and He is One who specializes in the impossible.

What Jonah experienced on that shore was not just an escape from the sea but a "resurrection from the dead." Three days after his apparent death, he arose from the sea, though still with a sin nature. Three days after He died, the Lord Jesus arose from the realm of the dead, still *without* a sin nature. By Jonah's "death" some men came to know the true God. By Jesus' death, God's love and salvation was made available to all people (John 3:16).

***

Father in heaven, we thank You for your precious Book, packed full, shaken together, and overflowing with marvels and mysteries we can never begin to imagine are possible.

Help us, dear Father, to be sensitive to what You are doing in Your world. Let us never sink to the level of saying to the living God of heaven and earth, "Lord, this is too much for You. I can't imagine it; therefore it cannot happen." Lord, rebuke us, and show us Your way so that we might be deeply taught how great You are. We ask it in Jesus' name. Amen.

③

JONAH AND THE GREAT FISH

Jonah 1:17 — 2:10

AS far as Jonah was concerned, God had consigned him to physical death as the righteous penalty for his deliberate disobedience to the will of God. As far as the sailors on that floating extension of the Bible Seminary of the Mediterranean were concerned, Jonah was dead and gone. But, miracle of miracles, God was doing things beneath the surface that human minds could not begin to imagine and that we will never comprehend fully until we meet the Lord someday. Then the hidden things of darkness will be brought to light. Then we will see as we are seen and know as we are known, and God will show us the really deep things He does in this world.

This statement has to be one of the most spectacular challenges to the naturalistic mind anywhere in Scripture:

> *Now the Lord had prepared a great*
> *fish to swallow Jonah. And Jonah*

61

> ***was in the belly of the fish three
> days and three nights.*** **(Jonah 1:17)**

First, there is a technical point here. The Lord
Jesus said that just as Jonah was three days and
three nights in the belly of the fish, so He
Himself would be "in the heart of the earth," in
Sheol/Hades, for three days and three nights
(Matthew 12:40). Yet the New Testament makes
it rather clear that He was *not* there three full
days and nights. He was there only one *full* day.
He was crucified on Friday and died that af-
ternoon at 3:00, at which moment He entered
Sheol/Hades to announce His victory over Satan.
He remained there through the Sabbath Day,
Saturday, and rose early on Sunday morning.
How, then, could He say He would be in the
heart of the earth *three* days and *three* nights?

The Old Testament gives us a clue as to how
the Jews considered the term *day*. A day and a
night, in the light of Genesis 1, is normally a se-
quence of twenty-four hours. But when speaking
of days, the Old Testament historians counted
any part of a day as a full day. The clue to this
understanding is found in the book of Esther.

In her hour of crisis, when her life and the life
of her people were at stake, Queen Esther told
her cousin Mordecai,

> "Go, gather all the Jews who are present in Shushan, and fast for me; neither eat nor drink for three days, night or day. My maids and I will fast likewise. And so I will go to the king, which is against the law; and if I perish, I perish!" So Mordecai went his way and did according to all that Esther commanded him.
>
> Now it happened on the third day that Esther put on her royal robes and stood in the inner court of the king's palace. (Esther 4:16–5:1)

Esther entered the king's palace "on the third day," which would have been before the three days and nights of fasting were completed *if* those were complete days. In the same way, Jesus rose on the "third day" (Matthew 16:21; 17:23; 20:19; 1 Corinthians 15:4), before three full twenty-four-hour periods had passed, indicating that parts of three days and three nights were counted as three full days and three full nights.

Jonah probably was in the belly of the fish less than three full twenty-four-hour days, but he was there sufficiently long for him to have died. No human being could possibly survive under the ocean for even thirty minutes. Yet somehow he was miraculously preserved from death inside that amazing organic submarine, which carried him to the Holy Land and disgorged him on the shore (Jonah 2:10). I am convinced that in the perfectly calm sea God miraculously provided, Jonah arrived on the shore of the Holy Land before the ship did. God, the Lord, Creator of heaven and earth, prepared this great fish to swallow Jonah.

As a new convert at Princeton University in 1943, when the Lord by His grace brought me into His family, one of the first issues I faced was how to win fellow students and professors to the Lord. God gave me a great burden and desire to see people come to Christ, but I was extremely ignorant of God's ways and His Word. I just assumed that the only way to get intellectuals into God's kingdom is with superior intellectual arguments. Thus, through rational debate you can overwhelm their so-called proofs against the truth of Scripture with greater proofs for its truth. One day my spiritual father, Dr. Donald Fullerton, through whom I came to know the Lord, took me to one of the dorms to invite a student to our Sunday afternoon Bible class in the student center. I was not at all confident we would be successful, for I had been rejected repeatedly in my efforts to convert people, not realizing that God alone saves people through

His Word and that finite pressure on depraved minds is worse than worthless.

We knocked on the door. It slowly opened, and cigarette smoke poured out. We thought we saw in the murky darkness six or seven people. We stated the purpose of our being there was to invite a particular student to our Bible class at Murray Dodge Hall because he had signed our invitation form, saying that he wanted to come (maybe to prove to his parents that Princeton wasn't all that bad). Of course, then, with the pressure of assignments and dozens of other activities, the Princeton Evangelical Bible class was pushed down to the lowest level of priority, and he never came.

Now, in my opinion, Dr. Fullerton was one of the greatest missionaries to university students in the history of this country. He carried on his ministry at Princeton for fifty years, with a deep knowledge of the Lord, His Word, and His ways. This student, obviously, was extremely upset and embarrassed in the presence of his classmates in that dormitory room. He said, "Gentlemen, I'm very sorry. I am not interested in coming to a Bible class anymore." I felt like saying, "Sorry we bothered you." But Dr. Fullerton very graciously and with a smile, asked, "Why are you not interested in studying God's

Word?" The student said, "I've been here four months, and I've discovered that the Bible is not true." Dr. Fullerton did not take that at face value, however; he knew there was something beneath that. He said, "You've been here four months. What have you discovered about the Bible that has convinced you it is not true?" Of course, that was the last thing the student wanted to be confronted with, because, obviously, he had made no particular discoveries about the Bible.

Frequently across this nation the same thing happens. Students who come from quasi-conservative religious backgrounds go to major secular institutions of academic and scientific studies, and they soon discover that in these places very few take the Bible seriously. It is not quoted, little is done in the light of this Book, and the God of this Book is rarely honored or mentioned. The really *cool* thing is to ignore the Bible totally, and thus minds are transformed as they are engulfed in secularism, materialism, and despair.

This student was now trapped. What was he going to say? He blurted out, "Jonah and the whale—who could ever believe such a silly story? It is scientifically and historically absurd." He said the wrong thing to the wrong person.

Providentially, I was prevented from speaking at that point. I was going to say, "If that is your problem, give us a few weeks. We'll go to the library and find books that will show you that whales do have mouths big enough to swallow people, and, as matter of fact, we have historical records available to show that people have been swallowed and lived to tell of it." I am so thankful God prevented me from saying that, because that was the last thing this young man needed.

The other students were gathered around listening now, and I was in a state of great perplexity. Dr. Fullerton said, "I am so thankful that you mentioned the book of Jonah, one of the most fascinating books in the entire Bible, especially in the light of what Jesus Christ the Lord said about it. If we had time, I'd love to sit down with you and discuss these mysteries and marvels. But before I do this, let me tell you how I came to know that everything in this Book is true. I was a student here myself thirty years ago, and I couldn't possibly have been less interested in God and His Word. But finally, God brought me to the bottom, and the only direction I had to look was up. He met me in His grace and mercy through Jesus Christ the Lord, God's infinite and perfect love gift to the human race."

This godly man began to unfold the gospel. He did not argue about history or science. He simply presented God's infallible and inerrant Word, which is self-authenticating and uniquely guaranteed by the Holy Spirit to drive deep conviction into human hearts that possess the image and likeness of God, even if they do not know it. Dr. Fullerton operated on certain presuppositions; namely, that unsaved people are blind and that mere human logic cannot penetrate the depth of their need. In just thirty minutes, he graciously and effectively unfolded the marvels of God's plan for salvation. Within one hour, that student was on his knees, acknowledging Jesus Christ as his Lord and Savior.

I could not believe this. I went up to him and said, "But what about Jonah and the fish?" He said, "I don't have the faintest idea about the book of Jonah, but now I have come to believe that whatever God has said in His Book must be true."

That is called regeneration. It is a spiritual miracle whereby the anointing of the Holy One enables us to enter into a realm of spiritual truth where we do not need experts to "permit" us to believe. We do not need a great scholar to tell us we may now believe in Jesus and the truth of the Bible. The Spirit of God does a massive, inner work of transformation to bring us from darkness to light, from death to spiritual life (see John 16:7-11).

I have come to the conclusion that there is no valid evidence available that anyone in history has ever experienced what Jonah did. It was unique.

Likewise, I have checked out various reports about finding Noah's ark on the mountains of Ararat, and I have concluded that no one has found it. I was on a film a few years ago, broadcast nationwide by CBS, and I told the people who invited me to have a part in the film that I was not interested in doing it if they were going to insist that Noah's ark had been discovered. I am convinced that it has not been found and that all the rumors and contradictory reports are just that. Dr. John Morris of the Institute for Creation Research has been to that area several times and has officially stated that we have not really found the ark. I do not believe we ever will because in the church age God does not divert the attention of His people to miracle objects. He directs them only to His Word. I do not believe the Shroud of Turin is the final proof that Jesus died. I do not believe we are going to find the ark of the covenant. Indeed, Jeremiah 3:16 says that we will never find it.

One great miracle object the Old Testament talks about—namely, the brazen serpent—remained in Jerusalem for seven hundred years. Then King Hezekiah smashed it to pieces and called it *Nehushtan*, meaning simply, "a piece of brass," because it was misused by God's people as a fetish (2 Kings 18:4).

God wants us to trust Him and His Word. Jesus said, "Blessed are those who have not seen and yet have believed" (John 20:29). We are left with God's infallible, inerrant Word, the Bible. When we believe what God has said in the Bible, we are truly blessed.

God specially prepared a great fish. The One who created the universe with all the stars, galaxies, planets, and moons was perfectly capable of filling oceans with all the great sea monsters with one word. Thousands of kinds with marvelous, distinctive physical characteristics and functions were created instantly with no problem at all. God the Son, Jesus Christ, walked this earth less than two thousand years ago and instantly, by His mere word, created from water 150 gallons of genuine juice of grapes with the appearance of a history that it did not have. He was perfectly capable of taking loaves and fishes and creating ten thousand full-grown fishes that looked like they came fresh from the sea, hatched from eggs and caught by fishermen. They were created full-grown and dried, ready to eat, with an appearance of history.

Every sign-miracle the Creator of heaven and earth performed in His incarnate state was of this very nature. He gave sight to the blind, making it appear as though they had never been blind. He healed lepers, giving them the appearance that they had never been lepers. Lazarus came forth from the tomb, appearing as if he had never died. That is the hallmark of Christ the Lord. He created full-grown fruit trees laden with fruit—not seeds in the ground, but trees. He created the first humans as full-grown people—mature, functioning, sinless human beings with the appearance of a history they did not possess.

Jonah 1:17 is impossible to take seriously unless we know who Christ the Lord is and respect His written, infallible record and His infinite power and wisdom. Yet vastly more significant than preparing a great fish to swallow Jonah was the transformation the living God accomplished in the heart of Jonah. Preparing a fish was one thing; preparing a prophet to obey the Lord was something else. Creating the sun and moon was spectacular; getting you and me wrenched from the kingdom of darkness and into the kingdom of God's dear Son through the price of the shed blood of Christ on the cross is in an infinitely higher category of magnificence. The miracle with the fish at the conclusion of chapter 1, then, is not as significant as the prayer that was spoken inside the fish in chapter 2.

> *Then Jonah prayed to the Lord his God from the fish's belly.* **(Jonah 2:1)**

Jesus taught that "men always ought to pray and not lose heart" (Luke 18:1). No matter how deep or horrible the circumstances might be, they are simply a backdrop to the magnificence of God's grace in answering prayer in situations that seem totally hopeless. We will never regret the time we spent in prayer, but we may well regret that we did not pray enough. "Pray without ceasing" (1 Thessalonians 5:17). Acknowledge Him because He is in charge. He is directing, and He will guide and protect.

> *And he said: "I cried out to the Lord because of my affliction, and He answered me. Out of the belly of Sheol I cried, and You heard my voice."* **(Jonah 2:2)**

This sounds as if Jonah actually did die. "Out of the belly of Sheol" seems to suggest that he was in the place of departed spirits. However, what this really suggests is that Jonah had mastered the book of Psalms. The psalmist speaks along these same lines.

> The pangs of death surrounded me, and the floods of ungodliness made me afraid.
>
> The sorrows of Sheol surrounded me; the snares of death confronted me.
>
> In my distress I called upon the Lord, and cried out to my God; He heard my voice from His temple, and my cry came before Him, even to His ears. (Psalm 18:4-6)

David and other Old Testament saints described their crisis experiences as if they were actually in Sheol/Hades.

> For great is Your mercy toward me, and You have delivered my soul from the depths of Sheol. (Psalm 86:13)
>
> O Lord, God of my salvation, I have cried out day and night before You.
>
> Let my prayer come before You; incline Your ear to my cry.
>
> For my soul is full of troubles, and my life draws near to the grave.

> I am counted with those who go down
> to the pit; I am like a man who has no
> strength,
>
> Adrift among the dead, like the slain
> who lie in the grave, whom You re-
> member no more, and who are cut off
> from Your hand.
>
> You have laid me in the lowest pit, in
> darkness, in the depths.
>
> Your wrath lies heavy upon me, and
> You have afflicted me with all Your
> waves. (Psalm 88:1-7)

The author of Psalm 88 described the billows
of judgment, chastisement, and anger from God
that had flowed over him, and he cried from the
realm of the dead. He was not dead; he was simply saying that he might just as well be dead;
indeed, he was in a state worse than death. He
had displeased God and was under His hand of
heavy judgment.

As mentioned before, Jesus said that Jonah
was not dead. He said that during those three
days and three nights, Jonah was in the fish and
not in Sheol/Hades. So Jonah's statement must
be taken in the context of Old Testament poetry
as a figure of speech.

> *For You cast me into the deep, into*
> *the heart of the seas, and the*

> *floods surrounded me; all Your bil-*
> *lows and Your waves passed over*
> *me. ... The waters surrounded me,*
> *even to my soul; the deep closed*
> *around me; weeds were wrapped*
> *around my head. I went down to*
> *the moorings of the mountains; the*
> *earth with its bars closed behind*
> *me forever.* **(Jonah 2:3, 5-6a)**

Notice that Jonah said the Lord, not the sailors, cast him into the sea. His perspective was like Job's. Satan brought upon Job wave after wave of disaster, destroying his property, killing his children, and taking away his health so that even his wife told him, "Curse God and die!" (Job 2:9). But Job said, "The LORD gave, and the LORD has taken away; blessed be the name of the LORD" (Job 1:21). Job did not know about Satan, but it made no difference, because Satan disappeared from the rest of the book as an insignificant puppet pulled by invisible strings from the third heaven.

God, not Satan, is the One who is in control. Satan has no power whatever to do anything to God's people apart from the will and purpose of God. He is so feeble that the weakest saint can resist him in the name of the Lord and he will flee (see James 4:7). We do not have to come to grips with demons, name them, and cast them out. All we have to do is keep our eyes on the Lord, do His will, and appropriate the armor of defense (Ephesians 6), and Satan will be defeated by God's infallible Word. That is how spiritual warfare must be waged biblically.

Jonah understood that it was the sovereign Lord who had cast him into the sea. Jonah had his theology wonderfully straight, and this is reflected in his prayer; but his grasp of God's sovereign work did not come to him *after* he was thrown overboard. The way to have an effective "foxhole prayer experience" is to prepare for it long in advance. You do not become theologically alert and biblical at the moment the crisis comes, after neglecting God and His Word for years.

I often think of the apostle Peter in Matthew 14. At Jesus' command, He stepped out of the boat and walked on the water, the only mere human ever to do so. Momentarily, as Peter was walking on the water, he took his eyes off the Lord. I imagine that he became thrilled as he looked at the amazing thing he was doing. Maybe he looked back to the eleven in the boat and said, "Hey, fellows, what do you think of this?" All of a sudden, down he went. Then came a prayer. It was no long, elaborate, involved discussion with Scripture references, but simply, "Lord, save me!" And the Lord did save him, because behind that desperate cry were years of knowledge, experience, and submission to God and His Word. When the crisis came, the prayer did not need to be all that long.

Jonah had much more time under the sea to pray than Peter did as he was sinking into the sea. In poetic language Jonah described the "deep" closing in around him as he sank ever deeper under the waves above.

How did Jonah ever get himself into such a situation? Jonah has a word of warning for us as we read his story. Whatever we do, we must never fight the living God. Nothing can be more terrifying than to be on the wrong end of a battle with God.

> Why do the nations rage, and the people plot a vain thing? The kings of the earth set themselves, and the rulers take counsel together, against the Lord and against His Anointed, saying, "Let us break Their bonds in pieces and cast away Their cords from us." (Psalm 2:1-3)

Such opposition to God is utterly foolish.

> He who sits in the heavens shall laugh; the Lord shall hold them in de-

> rision. Then He shall speak to them in His wrath, and distress them in His deep displeasure: "Yet I have set My King on My holy hill of Zion." (Psalm 2:4-6)

God wins.

Then Jesus replied:

> "I will declare the decree: The Lord has said to Me, 'You are My Son, today I have begotten You.'" (Psalm 2:7)

That occurred on resurrection day, when He was declared to be the Son of God with power through His resurrection from the dead (cf. Acts 13:33-37; Romans 1:4).

> "'Ask of Me, and I will give You the nations for Your inheritance, and the ends of the earth for Your possession. You shall break them with a rod of iron; You shall dash them to pieces like a potter's vessel.'" (Psalm 2:8-9)

That is Armageddon. I would not want to be on the receiving end of one word from Christ the Lord as He descends from heaven above in infinite dignity. All the armies of the world under the Beast will be waiting for Him to set foot on this planet so they can destroy Him—again. But it is the armies that will be destroyed in an instant, dashed "to pieces" (Revelation 19:11-21).

Jonah warns us: "Do not try it. You will find yourselves at the bottom of the world. You will be destroyed forever."

The one little thread that separated Jonah from the lake of fire was faith in his God.

> *"Then I said, 'I have been cast out of Your sight; yet I will look again toward Your holy temple.' ... Yet You have brought up my life from the pit, O Lord, my God. When my soul fainted within me, I remembered the Lord; and my prayer went up to You, into Your holy temple."* (Jonah 2:4, 6b-7)

Jonah's faith was expressed in his desire to "look again toward [the Lord's] holy temple." I used to wonder about that statement. How did he know which direction to look to find the temple? Which direction was east? But that is not what he was saying at all. Where is God's real temple? The original pattern for the tabernacle was given to Moses on Mount Sinai, and he built the earthly tabernacle according to that pattern. The real tabernacle/temple has always been *up there*. The temple in Jerusalem was a mere earthly expression of something even more real in the spiritual realm of the third heaven. It symbolized the means for depraved humans to approach a holy God. It illustrated that blood alone can take away the sin of the world. I have come to understand that the tabernacle/temple in the Old Testament, its future manifestation eschatologically on earth, and its invisible, original existence in heaven above shed tremendous light on what Jonah had in mind here.

Consider some of these statements that Jonah might have had in mind as he came to his hour of crisis.

> But as for me, I will come into Your house in the multitude of Your mercy; in fear of You I will worship toward Your holy temple. (Psalm 5:7)

> The Lord is in His holy temple, the Lord's throne is in heaven; His eyes behold, His eyelids test the sons of men. (Psalm 11:4)

> The pangs of death surrounded me, and the floods of ungodliness made me afraid.

> The sorrows of Sheol surrounded me; the snares of death confronted me.

> In my distress I called upon the Lord, and cried out to my God; He heard my voice from His temple, and my cry came before Him, even to His ears. (Psalm 18:4-6)

God has a temple where He manifests His glory and from whence He brings blessing and deliverance when He hears our prayers.

> Blessed is the man You choose, and cause to approach You, that he may dwell in Your courts. We shall be satisfied with the goodness of Your house, of Your holy temple. (Psalm 65:4)

> "But the Lord is in His holy temple. Let all the earth keep silence before Him." (Habakkuk 2:20)

I consider Psalm 27 the supreme passage in the Old Testament on the function and significance of the temple of God for His theocratic rule in Israel. Surely this is one of the favorite psalms of God's people through the centuries. It is a psalm of David. Here he rejoices in his great God:

> The Lord is my light and my salvation; whom shall I fear? The Lord is the strength of my life; of whom shall I be afraid? ... One thing I have desired of the Lord, that will I seek: that I may dwell in the house of the Lord all the days of my life, to behold the beauty of the Lord, and to inquire in His temple. (Psalm 27:1, 4)

But how much time did David actually spend in the earthly tabernacle/temple? Very little. He was the most ubiquitous warrior Israel ever knew, dashing from one country to another, smashing enemy armies, constantly wandering and fleeing from enemies. He was hardly ever home. Yet David said there was just one thing that he desired: to dwell in the house of the Lord. The knowledge that was in the heart of David was so profound that God called him "a man after My own heart" (Acts 13:22). But while his spirit was willing, his flesh was very weak. "A righteous man may fall seven times," but Scripture says God will lift him up (Proverbs 24:16). Nobody fell farther and deeper than David did. But he was a "one-thing" person.

I seem to be a "multi-thing" person. I have dozens of projects and problems to worry about. I can hear David saying, "Wait a minute! Just one thing is needful, and that is to 'dwell in the house of the Lord all the days of my life, to behold the beauty of the Lord and to inquire in His temple.'" That has to be the temple of the third heaven.

Jesus said Mary was a "one-thing" person also. Martha was a "many-thing" person, "distracted with much serving" (Luke 10:40). Jesus said to her,

> "Martha, Martha, you are worried and troubled about many things. But one thing is needed, and Mary has chosen that good part, which will not be taken away from her." (Luke 10:41-42)

That is the word of the Lord Jesus Christ to me, and perhaps to you.

Another "one-thing" person was Paul, who spoke of "forgetting those things which are behind and reaching forward to those things which are ahead" (Philippians 3:13). Paul said that there was one thing that was set before him: to do Christ's will.

Inside the fish, Jonah suddenly became a "one-thing" person; and it was only that kind of prophet who could ever face Nineveh. That prophet must have total dedication. He must not question God or argue with Him but rather worship, honor, and obey Him. He should not even consider the affliction or rejection to come. That was none of his business. The servant is not greater than his lord.

Inside the body of that marine mammal, heading rapidly back to the Holy Land, Jonah said, "I remembered the Lord; and my prayer went up to You, into Your holy temple" (Jonah 2:7).

May God speak to our hearts in the same manner. Whatever threats we have to our ministry, testimony, home, or family, we must set our hearts on Jesus Christ. When we meet Jonah someday on the other shore and say, "I have so many questions; tell me all the details of how it happened," I suspect he will say, "There is just one thing needful: Did you get the message of my book? I remembered the LORD and found Him in His holy, heavenly temple."

Jonah was one of the most successful preachers in the history of the world. But before he reached that pinnacle of success, God put this man through trials we cannot even begin to imagine. It was not until Jonah was deep in the sea and inside the fish that he remembered the Lord and prayed. Jonah's heart was in the right place at last.

> *"Those who regard vain idols forsake their faithfulness, but I will sacrifice to You with the voice of thanksgiving. That which I have vowed I will pay. Salvation is from the LORD."* **(Jonah 2:8-9 NASB)**

That was the best Jonah could do under the circumstances. Jews were to offer sacrifices to the Lord, and God was very precise about how

84

this was to be handled in His theocracy. People could not just offer anything they wanted, anywhere they wanted, whenever it was convenient. There were very clear restrictions and specific penalties for transgression of those guidelines. The psalmist put it this way:

> "Offer to God thanksgiving, and pay your vows to the Most High. Call upon Me in the day of trouble; I will deliver you, and you shall glorify Me." (Psalm 50:14-15)

I am sure Jonah had memorized that verse and was now putting it into effect. It was almost as if the psalmist were anticipating what the book of Jonah tells about this great prophet.

> "Whoever offers praise glorifies Me; and to him who orders his conduct aright I will show the salvation of God." (Psalm 50:23)

Animal sacrifices or any other offerings the Old Testament law required certainly would have been impossible for Jonah inside this fish. Yet even in the Old Testament era, the heart attitude was more important than the outward action (1 Samuel 15:22; Psalm 51:16-17). The New Testament tells us that we are to worship God "in spirit and truth" (John 4:24), recognizing that God Himself is Spirit and that the spiritual realities represented by material things are of greater importance than the symbols. No doubt Jonah would gladly have offered the required sacrifices had he been able to, and he was determined to do so; but God wanted his heart, and now He had it.

Today God tells us to "offer the sacrifice of praise to God, that is, the fruit of our lips, giving thanks to His name" (Hebrews 13:15), coming from hearts that are regenerated and praising Him. That is the kind of sacrifice that truly pleases the Lord.

Jonah also promised, "That which I have vowed I will pay." Surely he knew of Solomon's dire warning: "When you make a vow to God, do not delay to pay it; for He has no pleasure in fools. Pay what you have vowed" (Ecclesiastes 5:4). In fact, the Bible says, if you really are not serious about keeping a vow, then you should not make one. God is very displeased with rash vows and insincere promises.

But what was Jonah's vow? I suspect that Jonah, in his heart of hearts, had said to the Lord in the depths of his crisis, "Lord, when I arrive back in my land, I am going to Nineveh. I hate the whole thought, for it is the opposite of my personal preferences; but my thoughts are not Your thoughts on that issue. I have vowed that if

You ever get me out of this place, I will do exactly what You have told me to do; and no matter what, I will keep my vow."

I am sure the tendency in my heart and yours is something like this: "Lord, I know You are watching and listening and keeping a record of my promises to You. Perhaps it will be safer not to make any." But we are trapped in both directions. God says, "You will devote your heart to Me, commit your life to Me long-term, promise Me that you will serve Me and do My will, and I will hold you to it." We are under tremendous pressure by a loving, gracious God to do what He knows is best for us in the light of eternity. We do not know what is best for us any more than children know what is best for them. We must trust our heavenly Father, who does know.

Jonah's experience inside the great fish ended with this profound statement: "Salvation is from the LORD." The prophet recognized that his deliverance could be effected only by the miraculous work of the Lord.

> *So the Lord spoke to the fish, and it vomited Jonah onto dry land.*
> **(Jonah 2:10)**

The only One who could save Jonah spoke to the fish He had prepared, and it cast Jonah out "onto dry land." The fish must have been absolutely thrilled when it vomited out this in-digestible passenger. It doubtless flipped its tail and went away happily, not fully realizing its unique experience.

***

Father, speak to our hearts on this day. Many times we think we are sinking into the depths, and many have given up the ministry because they don't see in the land of the living, the hand of the living God. May we trust You as never before and say, "Lord, there are some things that are Your business, and there are some things that You have entrusted to us to be our business. Help us to sort out what is really important and do the things that really count for eternity: worshiping You, praising You, and honoring You in Your holy temple." We ask this in Jesus' name. Amen.

JONAH IN NINEVEH

Jonah 3:1-10

> *Now the word of the Lord came to*
> *Jonah the second time, saying ...*
> **(Jonah 3:1)**

THANK the Lord for these "second times" and for not casting us off when we disobey Him. We do not deserve a second opportunity, either to hear the gospel or to obey and do His will. But how gracious and long-suffering He is!

Peter the apostle had a "second time." He was by the Sea of Galilee with six other disciples of Jesus. Jesus had risen from the dead, and they had seen Him; but they were very discouraged men, not knowing what to do or where to go. So they went fishing. But then they saw Jesus on the shore; and when they came to Him, He had breakfast prepared. Then He looked at Peter, eye to eye, and said, "Simon, son of Jonah, do you love Me more than these?" (John 21:15). Before the crucifixion, Peter had indicated that he loved Jesus more than any of the other men and declared that no matter what others did, he would never fall away or deny Jesus (Matthew 26:31-35). Peter did not know his own heart, for he proceeded to deny Jesus three times, just as Jesus foretold (Matthew 26:69-75).

Peter had been devastated by his denial of Christ, but now the Lord said, "Tend My sheep" (John 21:16). Here was Peter's second chance to obey the Lord. There were people out there to be taught, discipled, and sent forth to the ends of the earth. The flock needed to be fed, and Jesus was calling Peter to feed them. What an opportunity God gave to Peter to vindicate his faith in the Lord Jesus and vindicate himself after the awful nightmare of his denial!

Saul of Tarsus also experienced a second opportunity and the gracious forgiveness of Jesus on the road to Damascus, when Jesus said to him, "Saul, Saul, why are you persecuting Me? It is hard for you to kick against the goads" (Acts 26:14). He never forgot that. In 1 Corinthians 15:9, he wrote, "For I am the least of the apostles, who am not worthy to be called an apostle, because I persecuted the church of God." His previous persecution of believers haunted him as long as he lived, but he could still declare, "By the grace of God I am what I am" (verse 10). Surely Jonah could share that sentiment and say,

"I am here in a ministry to Nineveh by the grace of God alone, not by my scheming."

How did Jonah hear the word of God? That is one of the unresolved mysteries of the Old Testament. Over and over again, the Bible says, the Lord *spoke* to Jonah. Did He speak in an audible voice or as a theophany, appearing as a man, as perhaps Adam and Eve witnessed in the garden (Genesis 3:8)? Likewise, three men appeared to Abraham and Sarah one day, and we know one of them was the preincarnate Christ and the other two were angels (Genesis 18).

There is a great variety of ways in which God spoke to people in ages past. One of the most amazing things I have ever read is in Deuteronomy 30:11-14. There God gives us a clue as to the ultimate method by which He communicates to His servants. The apostle Paul quoted this passage in Romans 10:

> "Do not say in your heart, 'Who will ascend into heaven?'" (that is, to bring Christ down from above) or, "'Who will descend into the abyss?'" (that is, to bring Christ up from the dead). But what does it say? "The word is near you, in your mouth and in your heart" (that is, the word of faith which we preach). (Romans 10:6-8)

God created us in His image and likeness. As such, we have a unique combination of attributes that make us persons. We have a conscience, a will, an intellect, and a capacity for rational communication. There is an infinite chasm between man and beast that can never be bridged, but God speaks to the heart of man. As a result, He can say,

> If you confess with your mouth the Lord Jesus and believe in your heart that God has raised Him from the dead, you will be saved. (Romans 10:9)

Out of the heart of man come the issues of life (Proverbs 4:23), and out of the heart of man come evil thoughts and blasphemies (Matthew 15:18-19). That is where the action is. In His infinite wisdom and marvelous, mysterious ways, God could speak directly to the heart of Jonah and to every Old Testament prophet. In the same manner, we can be saved today, receive the light of the living God, and enter His kingdom and family, if our heart responds to His Word, which is illumined by the Holy Spirit. The Holy Spirit is the third Person the Godhead, and He specializes in communicating His will to you and me (cf. 1 Peter 1:10-12).

The "word of the LORD came to Jonah." There was nothing fuzzy here. Jonah got the message.

> *"Arise, go to Nineveh, that great city, and preach to it the message that I tell you."* **(Jonah 3:2)**

God told Jonah once again to go to Nineveh, "that great city." We heard that already in Jonah 1:2: "Go to Nineveh, that great city, and cry out against it; for their wickedness has come up before Me."

Let us face it: God deliberately makes the Great Commission impossible for us to fulfill in our wisdom and strength. "Without Me, you can do nothing" (John 15:5), Jesus said. All the programs, schemes, and organizations we employ, while useful and well-intentioned, can neglect the one thing that is needful: total submission to the Father, Son, and Holy Spirit, apart from Whom we can do absolutely nothing to convert anyone, improve the government, or change society. We are helpless apart from the eternal, triune God. He deliberately pushes us, just as he pushed Jonah, into a corner where we must admit that it is impossible. He wants us to get the message that the only way anything that honors God and lasts forever can be done is if God does it through us and in spite of us.

God got the message to Nineveh in spite of Jonah. His resistance, rationalizing, emotions, and perspectives all had to be smashed before Nineveh ever heard anything. Here is God's lesson for us: Never give up. Be patient. God is not through with us either. He wants to show us all more and more of His majesty and power. The Word He has given us is totally sufficient in itself. It is infinite and eternal and will outlast the universe. It does not need finite props or human help to make it credible and acceptable to human hearts.

God called Nineveh a "great city." And in the last verse of the book, He told us how great it was.

> "And should I not pity Nineveh, that great city, in which are more than one hundred and twenty thousand persons who cannot discern between their right hand and their left—and much livestock?" (Jonah 4:11)

Most commentaries agree that this verse refers to children younger than the so-called age of accountability; that is, those who cannot tell the difference between right and wrong. That would mean the city probably was home to 600,000 people at a minimum. Sending one man to a city of 600,000 people might seem strange, but God specializes in one-man armies. The formula is "Let God be true but every man a liar" (Romans 3:4). One man with God is the majority. Ask the nation of Israel about a man called Elijah—a one-man army. He absolutely terrified the king of Israel (cf. 1 Kings 18:17). Noah was a one-man army through whom, according to Hebrews 11, the whole world was condemned—not just a city but the entire human race.

On the basis of the genealogical information in Genesis 5, Dr. Henry Morris mathematically calculated the minimal population of the world by the time of the Flood. In Genesis 5, the formula looks like this:

> ___ lived ___ years and begot ___.
> After he begot ___, he lived ___ years,
> and had sons and daughters. So all the
> days of ___ were ___; and he died.

That means that each man had to have at least five children. Multiply that by the number of years that elapsed between Creation and the Flood, remembering that people probably lived hundreds of years of overlapping generations. Thus, the population of this planet had to be at least one billion by the time of the Flood. That would mean there was one teacher for a billion people. The congregation to whom God sent Noah is described in Genesis 6:5:

> Then the Lord saw that the wicked-
> ness of man was great in the earth,
> and that every intent of the thoughts
> of his heart was only evil continually.

What an assignment!

> By faith Noah, being divinely warned
> of things not yet seen, moved with
> godly fear, prepared an ark for the
> saving of his household, by which he
> condemned the world and became
> heir of the righteousness which is ac-
> cording to faith. (Hebrews 11:7)

The only real difference between Noah and
Jonah was that everybody Jonah preached to repented. No one that Noah preached to, outside
his own family, repented. But that was God's
plan (see Isaiah 55:8-11). People's response is not
our prerogative or responsibility. That takes an
enormous burden off the shoulders of the missionary, pastor, or parent. We do what God says.
We hear and proclaim His Word without compromise, in love accompanied by prayer, but
only God can produce the spiritual fruit and
bring the necessary response (John 15:4).

God sent Jonah to Nineveh, and He would
teach the prophet something about the power of
His word. Notice, the Lord told Jonah, "Preach
... the message that I tell you" (Jonah 3:2). There

were to be no additions, no subtractions, no revisions. Jonah was to speak exactly what God told him to speak.

God perfectly designed this Book we call the Bible in Hebrew, Aramaic, and Greek. In the autographs, this Book is absolutely perfect, inerrant, and infallible—God-breathed. God says if we add anything to His Word, He will add to us the plagues that are written in it. If we subtract from it, He will take away our part from the Book of Life (Revelation 22:18-19). I do not know exactly what that means, but I have decided not to add to it or subtract from it! All we need is His Word, and if it is not supremely honored, vigorously set forth before a godless world, and watched over with constant prayer, we will be in deep trouble.

God wasn't asking for Jonah's imaginary improvements and additions. God was simply telling Jonah to proclaim to the people of Nineveh what the Lord was telling him. Jonah knew what David said in Psalm 3:1-6:

> Lord, how they have increased who trouble me! Many are they who rise up against me.
>
> Many are they who say of me, "There is no help for him in God."

> But You, O Lord, are a shield for me,
> my glory and the One who lifts up my
> head.
>
> I cried to the Lord with my voice, and
> He heard me from His holy hill.
>
> I lay down and slept; I awoke, for the
> Lord sustained me.
>
> I will not be afraid of ten thousands of
> people who have set themselves
> against me all around.

The unknown author of Psalm 91 expressed a similar thought:

> A thousand may fall at your side, and
> ten thousand at your right hand; but it
> shall not come near you. (Psalm 91:7)

Nothing can ever destroy you when you are in God's will. You are a one-man army, completely protected by vast numbers of guardian angels. You are watched over by God the Father, God the Son, and God the Holy Spirit. And even though Satan may have an army of 200 million demons (Revelation 9:16), he is totally helpless in the presence of a servant of God who knows how to appeal to Him.

Michael the archangel was challenged one day with regard to the disposal of the body of Moses, which was buried east of the Dead Sea in a place unknown to man (Deut. 34:6). Satan appeared and demanded the body so that he could desecrate it. He hated Moses as one of the greatest instruments God ever had and the means by which the theocracy was launched following the exodus from Egypt.

I imagine the conversation went something like this: Michael looked at Satan and said, "I'm sorry, you cannot have this body." Satan said, "I told you to step aside; I am taking that body." Michael replied, "You may not have it. I have been stationed here to protect it from you." Satan said, "You don't know who I am, do you, Michael? I am the greatest angel in the universe, and the whole world is mine. I'm telling you to step aside now." To this challenge, Michael replied: "The Lord rebuke you!" (Jude 9). In other words, he was saying, "I can't handle you, Satan. You are superior, but I know Someone greater than you, and I'm turning you over to Him. I'm turning you over to the living God." That was the end of the confrontation.

We have the same resource Michael did. We can declare to people, "If you do not repent absolutely and unconditionally on God's terms, you will face His final judgment. That is divine authority, friends, spoken through tears and a broken heart and in genuine love. That may sound vindictive, but we know from the New Testament that love is doing for someone what is best for that person in the light of eternity, no matter what the price or cost may be to us. If we really love people, we will not compromise God's Word. We will tell them what God actually said so that they can see the whole picture and might repent of their sin and be converted and saved forever. That is love (cf. 1 John 4:7-20).

> *So Jonah arose and went to Nineveh, according to the word of the Lord.* (Jonah 3:3a)

Jonah had a new motivation and perspective. Now he was finally awakened to the fact that unless he operated his ministry according to the word of the Lord, nothing would ever happen, and he would be in enormous trouble with God.

Even when the beloved Son of God, the Lord Jesus Christ, walked the earth, He said over and over again that the things He said were not of Himself but what the Father told Him to say. (see John 8:26-28; 12:49; 15:15). He told His Father in John 17:14: "I have given them Your word." The Lord Jesus set the model for a perfect minister and instrument of the living God. We are to do exactly what God said whether we understand it or not and whether we like it or not. This is perhaps the hardest thing in Christian ministry we will ever have to learn.

> *Now Nineveh was an exceedingly great city, a three-day journey in extent.* **(Jonah 3:3b)**

Nineveh actually was a complex of cities—a great city with satellite cities—much like greater New York City today with all of its suburbs and smaller cities all integrated and interrelated with each other. It was an enormous complex of human population and governmental power. The description of Nineveh as a "three-day journey in extent" probably means Jonah went up one street and down another in a zigzag pattern, and by the time three days had passed, the whole complex of cities called Nineveh had heard the message God had sent him to proclaim.

> *And Jonah began to enter the city on the first day's walk. Then he cried out and said, "Yet forty days, and Nineveh shall be overthrown!"* **(Jonah 3:4)**

The word *overthrown* is used especially of what God did to Sodom and Gomorrah, those cities of the plain located at the southern end of the Dead Sea. Genesis 19:25 and 29 and Deuteronomy 29:23 say that God "overthrew" those cities. In Isaiah 13:19, God said that what He is going to do to Babylon some day is like what He did when He overthrew Sodom and Gomorrah.

God did not give any reason, explanation, or promise at all regarding how things would turn out when He sent Jonah to Nineveh. But it is fascinating that God said that in *forty days* Nineveh would be overthrown.

There was another time in human history when forty days were associated with divine judgment. It was phase one of the mountain-covering, yearlong, catastrophe of water called the Genesis Flood. For the first time in the history of the world, water fell from the heavens above and rose from the oceans beneath (Genesis 7:17).

Before those forty days of rain began, animals—two of each kind of bird, mammal, and reptile—had been led by God's unseen hand into the sole place of refuge on planet Earth; namely, the ark (Genesis 7:7-9). That surely struck terror into the hearts of millions who had heard the preaching of Noah and seen that great visual aid developing step by step on a high plateau.

First Peter 3:20 says, "The Divine longsuffering waited in the days of Noah, while the ark was being prepared." People everywhere heard, watched, and laughed at Noah's ark project. In 2

Peter 2:5 we are told that Noah was not only the ark builder but also a "preacher of righteousness," declaring a message from God. My opinion is that by the time the long-suffering of God came to an end after one hundred and twenty years (Genesis 6:3), everybody in the world had heard the warning and had laughed it to scorn. But then, all of a sudden, the laughter ended, as people saw animals moving to the ark. They must have been gripped with terror, thinking that somehow these creatures had a premonition of a global catastrophe. The people probably fled to the hills to escape what they surely thought was a quirk of nature that would be temporary and limited in extent. But the higher they climbed, the higher the water rose, and they were picked off by the thousands and millions. In forty days—and probably less—every human being in the world had drowned except for the eight people inside the ark.

But think about this. Is it not possible that during that forty days of final probation of the antediluvian world, that some people, as they were drowning in the Flood, repented and believed before they died? It is never too late for people to repent and believe. The thief on the cross is one example of this. He could never survive the crucifixion, but he could be saved

(Luke 23:40-43). So we might wonder whether there were people floating around or possibly pounding on the door of the ark, saying, "Noah, let us in! We believe! You are right! We repent!" Their repentance could have been genuine, but it could not save them from death by drowning.

At the beginning of the Flood, it rained forty days and forty nights. God gave Israel forty years in the wilderness. That number forty is fascinating, especially as it relates to judgment.

"Forty days, and Nineveh shall be overthrown," Jonah proclaimed. It is probable the prophet had more to say than the brief excerpt recorded here. We know that in the book of Acts, only portions of the apostles' sermons are recorded. How big would the Bible be if each sermon was written down in its entirety? Whatever else was included in Jonah's message, it was enough that people could actually repent.

There may well have been something else that confirmed Jonah's message and made it especially effective. Jesus said something in the gospel of Luke that is not revealed anywhere else in the New Testament.

> "This is an evil generation. It seeks a sign, and no sign will be given to it except the sign of Jonah the prophet. For as Jonah became a sign to the

Ninevites, so also the Son of Man will
be to this generation." (Luke 11:29-30)

Jesus emerged from the heart of the earth
with the marks of crucifixion still on His hands
and feet. Surely the sacrificial Lamb of God will
bear those signs forever to remind us of the price
He paid for you and me on the cross. In a similar
way, Jesus' words in Luke suggest that Jonah
was a *sign* to Nineveh because the people could
see something about him that confirmed what
they had heard. This man had been to the bottom of the Mediterranean and lived to tell the
story of what God had told him, and now he
was delivering the message God had entrusted
to him. Many scholars have concluded that the
many hours inside the belly of the fish changed
Jonah's complexion forever. The man must have
looked horrible, but as such, he was a sign to the
Ninevites. Thus, when Jonah proclaimed that
their doom was sealed, the message had a tremendous impact and brought about an amazing
event.

> *So the people of Nineveh believed
> God, proclaimed a fast, and put on
> sackcloth, from the greatest to the
> least of them. Then word came to
> the king of Nineveh; and he arose
> from his throne and laid aside*

> *his robe, covered himself with*
> *sackcloth and sat in ashes.* **(Jonah**
> **3:5-6)**

This was astounding! That wicked city repented and believed in the God of Jonah. It is easy to underestimate the power of God's Word as we sow the seed and proclaim its message day after day; but the eternal destiny of the human race hangs on how they respond to the message God has entrusted to you and me. Yes, "with God all things are possible" (Matthew 19:26). Here is one thing that was not just possible but was actual—the city of Nineveh believed in God. Jesus Himself confirmed Nineveh's repentance as an historical fact:

> "The men of Nineveh will rise up in
> the judgment with this generation and
> condemn it, for they repented at the
> preaching of Jonah; and indeed a
> greater than Jonah is here." (Luke
> 11:32)

As seemingly impossible as it might appear, Jesus said it happened. In fact, it happened so thoroughly and deeply that we are almost overwhelmed by the magnitude of this repentance. It was citywide and, presumably, almost nationwide, because not only did the people call a fast and put on sackcloth, but upon hearing of Jonah's message, the king also participated, putting on sackcloth and sitting in ashes.

These acts were standard visual aids, outward expressions of inward repentance and self-humiliation. When God allowed everything Job had to be taken away and his body to be afflicted, he sat in ashes (Job 2:8). When Daniel made confession for his people, he did so with "fasting, sackcloth, and ashes" (Daniel 9:3-4). Not only did the king of Nineveh humble himself in sackcloth and ashes, but he also issued a proclamation.

And he caused it to be proclaimed and published throughout Nineveh by the decree of the king and his nobles, saying,

Let neither man nor beast, herd nor flock, taste anything; do not let them eat, or drink water. But let man and beast be covered with sackcloth, and cry mightily to God; yes, let everyone turn from his evil way and from the violence that is in his hands. Who can tell if God will turn and relent, and turn away from His

*fierce anger, so that we may
not perish?* (Jonah 3:7-9)

How could a king tell everybody in his capital city, if not his entire kingdom, to repent to a foreign God, the God of Israel and Jonah? We are already slightly prepared for this by the response of a group of pagan sailors, each of whom had his own god on the ship. God is able to do things we can hardly imagine. In fact, He specializes in just this kind of thing.

In 2 Chronicles 20:3 we find Jehoshaphat, a godly king of Judah, responding in a similar way when there was a great invasion of his nation. He called on the whole nation to fast and plead with God almighty to spare them. That was the only way the theocracy was ever intended by God to be defended, protected, and to survive against its enemies. There was no need for superior skills, tactics, maneuvers, and weapons, which is the world's way.

By the way, the "world's way" is the right way for a nation to defend itself today. I have visited West Point and seen the tomb of my father there in the cemetery. He was trained at West Point to believe with all his heart that the only possible way for this nation to survive in this kind of world is to have a superior army. Jesus said the same thing.

108

> Jesus answered, "My kingdom is not
> of this world. If My kingdom were of
> this world, My servants would fight,
> so that I should not be delivered to the
> Jews; but now My kingdom is not
> from here." (John 18:36)

However, the Jewish nation was special. It was not at all like the United States. Israel was God's chosen people, and their nation was a special, God-inaugurated, God-programmed theocracy. God said the way they were going to survive was by spiritual means. So at Jericho they had priests blowing trumpets. What kind of tactic was that? It was God's program, and He guaranteed that Judah and Israel would survive only to the extent that they did God's things God's way. (Jericho never recovered from those trumpets and the prayers that went with them!)

Jehoshaphat realized there was no use in trying to fight; so he said, "Let's just pray" (cf. 2 Chronicles 20:1-30). Hezekiah did the same thing when he received a threat from Sennacherib, the king of Assyria. Hezekiah simply opened Sennacherib's letter before the Lord (2 Kings 19). God's response was to supernaturally destroy the whole Assyrian army of 185,000 men in one night.

That miraculous deliverance occurred some eighty years after the time of Jonah and after

Nineveh recovered from its repentance and abject submission to God. The Assyrians returned to their arrogance and incomparable cruelty, and God did to Sennacherib what He could have done to the Assyrian king of Jonah's day a generation or two earlier. God certainly had the power to handle Nineveh in terms of judgment, but He is also a gracious God. From Genesis to Revelation, the Bible reveals God not only as the Creator and Maintainer of the universe and the One who wipes out wicked people, as in the Genesis Flood, but also as the One who redeems people who simply repent of their sin, and turn to Him. Jonah's day was not the time for God's judgment. God was going to do something very special that Jonah never fully fathomed.

We notice something quite strange about the repentance in Nineveh. Not only the people but also the beasts were going to repent! The book of Joel, written by a prophet who could have been contemporary with Jonah, records this statement about beasts, when God brought disaster upon the nation during its time of apostasy:

> How the animals groan! The herds of cattle are restless, because they have no pasture; even the flocks of sheep suffer punishment. O Lord, to You I cry out; for fire has devoured the open pastures, and a flame has burned all

110

> the trees of the field. The beasts of the
> field also cry out to You, for the water
> brooks are dried up, and fire has
> devoured the open pastures. (Joel
> 1:18-20)

God cursed the world because of man's sin. Romans 8 explains that the whole creation was "subjected to futility, not willingly"—not because of some inherited evolutionary defect—"but because of Him who subjected it in hope; because the creation itself also will be delivered from the bondage of corruption into the glorious liberty of the children of God" (Romans 8:20-21).

> For we know that the whole creation
> groans and labors with birth pangs
> together until now. Not only that, but
> we also who have the firstfruits of the
> Spirit, even we ourselves groan within
> ourselves, eagerly waiting for the
> adoption, the redemption of our body.
> (Romans 8:22-23)

That redemption will happen when the kingdom age comes and we are glorified. The whole animal kingdom will be released from its bondage, and lions will eat straw again like oxen, as they did at the dawn of earth's history (Isaiah 11:6-9). Animals suffer because of people who have rebelled against God. They are a spectacular visual aid to what the curse of God does to a beautiful world when people, who bear God's image and likeness, are out of harmony with Him.

We do not know precisely what the king of Assyria was thinking, but we know from ancient historical records that people in the ancient Near East really believed there is a biotic rapport between men and larger domestic animals, who suffer because of man's sin. It seems the king believed that covering the animals with sackcloth, thus "afflicting" them, would somehow appease God's wrath.

God is, in fact, interested in animals—though not like animal rights activists or evolutionists, who believe we are related to animals and not inherently superior to them. Notice that the book of Jonah ends with a comment about animals:

> And should I not pity Nineveh, that great city, in which are more than one hundred and twenty thousand persons who cannot discern between their right hand and their left—and much livestock?" (Jonah 4:11)

God created this world. He created trees, flowers, birds, mammals, and reptiles, as well as people. Everything in the universe is designed by God to reflect His glory and to be visual aids to encourage human beings to honor and acknowledge Him.

> *Then God saw their works, that*
> *they turned from their evil way;*
> *and God relented from the disaster*
> *that He had said He would bring*
> *upon them, and He did not do it.*
> **(Jonah 3:10)**

Jesus said to the self-righteous religious leaders of Israel, "Tax collectors and harlots enter the kingdom of God before you" (Matthew 21:31). Why was this the case? It was because the self-righteous would not come to repentance. Only people who know they are sinful are candidates for repentance. The person who thinks he is not so bad and is relatively superior, morally, intellectually, and ethically, is a prime candidate for God's judgment. He rejects God's evaluation that "all have sinned and fall short of the glory of God" (Romans 3:23) and that "the wages of sin is death" (Romans 6:23). Pride and arrogance, self-sufficiency, and suppression of God's perspectives guarantee eternal disaster. A city like Nineveh, which was notoriously wicked and cruel in its lifestyle, perspectives, and attitudes toward fellow human beings, was a ripe candidate for repentance.

But consider Israel and its capital, Samaria, and Judah and its capital, Jerusalem. They never did what Nineveh did. They never repented, and thus they were smashed by the Assyrians and the Babylonians. To this day, the reverberations of God's destruction on those cities—His cities in His land—continues. The ten northern tribes have never returned, and even Judah, from which we get the name *Jew*, is to this day a people who reject Jesus as Messiah. Because of this, God is even now preparing to bring upon the world the most horrible time human beings will ever know. It is called *The Great Tribulation* and *The Time of Jacob's Trouble*, and it is designed to bring the Jewish people to their knees in repentance, just as the Lord brought Nineveh to repentance. It will work, for all Israel, at last, will be saved (Romans 11:26).

Jonah tells us that "God relented" and did not bring judgment upon Nineveh. Does this mean God changed His mind? God is willing to take the risk, in terms of His reputation, for changing His mind. As we trace through the Bible, we find in Exodus 32 that God told Moses He was so horrified at what His people had done in worshiping a golden calf that He was going to wipe them all out and start again with Moses. Moses contended that God could not do this. His argument was, "What will the Egyptians say? What happened to Your promises? Your reputation will suffer irreparable damage." The text says, "So the Lord relented from the harm which He said He would do to His people" (Exodus 32:14).

Jeremiah wrote, "If that nation against whom I have spoken turns from its evil, I will relent of the disaster that I thought to bring upon it" (Jeremiah 18:8). Twice Amos pleaded with God not to destroy the nation. "So the Lord relented concerning this. 'It shall not be,' said the Lord" (Amos 7:3; cf. verse 6).

Of course, *God does not change His mind,* even though it may seem so from our finite, limited perspective! When Saul failed as the king of Israel, God told Samuel, "I regret that I have made Saul king" (1 Samuel 15:11 NASB; cf. verse 35). But then Samuel explained to Saul, "The Glory of Israel will not lie or change His mind; for He is not a man that He should change His mind" (1 Samuel 15:29 NASB; cf. Numbers 23:19; Psalm 110:4; Jeremiah 4:28; Malachi 3:6). There is no conflict between this statement and verses 11 and 35, where the Lord is said to "regret" that He had made Saul king. God's "regret" is simply an expresssion of real emotion, which is one of the marks of personality.

115

To Jonah this was potentially embarrassing, not just to God's reputation, but also to his. He was greatly grieved to think that God would send him on a mission to this wicked city to tell the people they had only forty days until the city was destroyed, and then the promised judgment did not come.

Here is another question that naturally arises from God's withdrawing His promised judgment on Nineveh: Were all these Ninevites who repented regenerated? That is, were they actually converted? Did they receive eternal life?

Consider this analogy. One of the worst kings who ever reigned in Israel was Ahab. In my opinion, he was worse than his wife Jezebel; at least you could count on her being wicked all the time.

When Ahab went out to see the vineyard his wife had acquired for him at the cost of Naboth's life, he admired the vines. But there in the vineyard, he was encountered by the prophet Elijah. Ahab said, "Have you found me, O my enemy?" (1 Kings 21:20). Elijah boldly told King Ahab that he was the enemy of the living God, for he had sold himself "to do evil in the sight of the Lord." As a result, the Lord would bring disaster upon Ahab and Jezebel and their whole household.

Ahab was shocked to the core and in total terror. The text says, "He tore his clothes and put sackcloth on his body, and fasted and lay in sackcloth, and went about mourning" (1 Kings 21:27). He performed the outward acts of repentance. God then said to Elijah:

> "See how Ahab has humbled himself before Me? Because he has humbled himself before Me, I will not bring the calamity in his days. In the days of his son I will bring the calamity on his house." (1 Kings 21:29)

I do not believe Ahab trusted the Lord and became a born-again, redeemed person. Rather, this was a temporary and superficial repentance. But if it was only superficial, why did God spare his kingdom? I suggest the answer is that at even the slightest sign of repentance under the threat of judgment, God shows mercy.

We must understand that not everybody who repents is saved eternally. Jesus told of a demon-possessed man who repented. The demon that had dwelt in him had gone out of him, but the man left his heart "empty, swept, and put in order" (Matthew 12:44). He was de-demonized, but he did not fill his heart with the Spirit of God and God's truth. So, Jesus said of the demon, "Then he goes and takes with him seven other spirits more wicked than himself, and they enter and dwell there; and the last state of that man is worse than the first" (Matthew 12:45).

Now let us look at the final words we have in the Bible about Ahab. Ahab asked Jehoshaphat, Judah's king, to join in a campaign against Ramoth Gilead. Ahab told Jehoshaphat to go into battle in his royal robes, but he, Ahab, would go into battle disguised. It seems Ahab had a deep suspicion that God was out to get him, and he thought he could fool the Lord. But an Assyrian soldier launched an arrow "at random," and it hit Ahab. God directed it right through the joints of the king's armor. As the chariot filled with blood, Ahab propped himself up, pretending to be fine, and creating an image to provide morale for his army. He was a courageous man, but he died (1 Kings 22; 2 Chronicles 18).

The clear impression we get from these and other Old Testament passages is that God is not mocked. Whatever we sow, we reap (Galatians 6:7). Ahab had repented temporarily and superficially, but he died under God's judgment. In God's unbelievable and astounding mercy and long-suffering toward people, He spared Nineveh—at least for a time.

***

Father in heaven, we stand absolutely astounded at what You have recorded in this precious Book. Lord, You are a God who specializes in hopeless, impossible situations. Without You, we can do nothing; yet with You and your precious Word that You have entrusted to us, all things are possible.

We who know You are Your children today because somebody prayed for us in years gone by. Perhaps with fear and trembling, that one also told us about Jesus, not knowing if there would be any response at all. Yet, here we are, as visible evidences that God can do the impossible. Apart from His grace, we would all be lost and heading for destruction that is eternal and deserved. O Lord, we thank You for your powerful and precious Word. In Jesus' name, we pray. Amen.

⑤

JONAH'S ANGER TOWARD GOD

Jonah 4:1-11

IT would have been nice if the book of Jonah had ended with chapter 3. However, there is one more chapter, and what we read there about Jonah is very disappointing.

> *But it displeased Jonah exceedingly, and he became angry. So he prayed to the Lord, and said, "Ah, Lord, was not this what I said when I was still in my country? Therefore I fled previously to Tarshish; for I know that You are a gracious and merciful God, slow to anger and abundant in lovingkindness, One who relents from doing harm.* **(Jonah 4:1-2)**

Jonah had done very well in his theological seminary courses in systematic theology. He probably had memorized God's statements to Moses that He is a merciful and gracious God, forgiving to a thousand generations people who repent and obey Him (Exodus 34:6-7; Deuteronomy 7:9). And that is exactly why Jonah did not want to go to Nineveh.

Jonah knew that since God warned the inhabitants of Nineveh forty days in advance of divine judgment, there was the possibility they would repent and God would forgive them. Jonah must have recognized immediately that this situation was very different from that of Sodom. The only people in Sodom who got any warning were those who were about to marry Lot's daughters, and they mocked Lot as if he were out of his mind (Genesis 19:14). Then the city collapsed under the fire of God from heaven (Genesis 19:24-25).

Nineveh received a warning, however, and when God gives a warning in Scripture, it always implies there is hope that those who have been warned will believe and act in the light of the warning. Thus, the warning to Nineveh left open the possibility that the people would repent and thereby receive what only God can give in the midst of depravity: forgiveness. Jonah wanted no part of such mercy. This is why he had fled toward Tarshish.

One of the most spectacular words in the Old Testament is *kesed*, translated "lovingkindness" in Jonah 4:2. This word refers to God's loyalty to His covenant promises, which are ultimately based upon the blood of His own beloved Son shed upon the cross. It is only on the basis of Christ's sacrifice that God can forgive people when they simply repent and believe in Him.

Jonah knew God is "abundant in loving-kindness," but he seemed to think that God did not fully realize the Israelites hated the Assyrians! Jonah could imagine what would happen to him if he returned to his homeland to report that the city of Nineveh was doing fine, that the Assyrians had responded to Jonah's message, and that God had withdrawn His threatened punishment. Jonah was concerned for his reputation. It would be much better for him and his future ministry back in Israel if he could just tell his people he had gone to Nineveh and denounced them in the name of the living God, and God had destroyed them all. Oh, how spectacular Jonah's testimony and popularity would be! There would be many opportunities and open doors for ministry!

Sometimes we fall into the trap of doing things for God in order to make doors open that God has not seen fit to open. We get pushy and manipulative with human schemes. But when God shuts a door, no one can open it; and when God opens a door, no one can close it (cf. Revelation 3:7). We need to be sensitive to that.

We want success, effectiveness, and fruitfulness in life and ministry. But the minute we start manipulating situations and people to accomplish what *we* want for ourselves, we fail. Someday Christians will answer to the living God at the *bema*, or judgment seat, of Christ, when everything we have ever done that is not in accordance with His will and way will evaporate like wood, hay, and stubble before the One whose eyes are like a flame of fire. The only things that will survive the *bema* are gold, silver, and precious stones (1 Corinthians 3:12-15); that is, those things done in obedience to His Word, no matter what the cost.

Jonah was saying, "Oh, Lord, I just can't handle the way You do things. I am very angry." Jesus gave a parable once about some angry people. A landowner hired them in the morning to work in his vineyard, and they agreed on the wages for the day. As the day went on, the vineyard owner hired other workers, including a few just before sunset. When pay time came, the master gave everybody exactly the same wages. The people who had worked all day said, "This is unfair. We worked in the heat of the day, and here are people you just hired, and you are giving them the same wage." The master answered, "Why should you be angry? Didn't I give you a job and pay you exactly what I promised? Are you angry because I am gracious to others?" (Matthew 20:15).

Jesus told us about another angry man. His younger brother, a prodigal son, finally came home, and his father rushed out to welcome him. He gave his returned son a feast with the fatted calf, the best robe, and a ring. The older brother saw all this and had evil thoughts in his heart: "I've served faithfully in this house and never gone out and wasted my father's money. Now he gets a feast and I don't." His father rebuked him with a broken heart (Luke 15:11-32). The message is this: Who are we to tell God to whom He should or should not show mercy? Who are we to tell God what He should do with His blessings? If God gave us what we deserved, we would all be doomed. We should thank the Lord for whatever blessings we have been given and spend all eternity thanking Him that He included us at all.

Do we have evil hearts about God's grace, mercy, love, and patience? Are there people on this planet whom we wish God would strike dead immediately? Yet God enables them to breathe His air, drink His water, and eat His food, even as they blaspheme Him. This is very hard for us to handle. The psalmist acknowledged the dilemma but also saw where the answer was found:

> For I was envious of the boastful, when I saw the prosperity of the wicked. ... When I thought how to understand this, it was too painful for me—until I went into the sanctuary of God; then I understood their end. (Psalm 73:3, 16-17)

In the temple of God—that is, in the presence of God and His Word—the whole thing becomes clearer. This little time on earth is not where God's blessing is fully demonstrated, but rather in the life to come. This is a probation time, a time when God extends mercy to people so that they might somehow turn to Him.

> *Therefore now, O Lord, please take my life from me, for it is better for me to die than to live!"* **(Jonah 4:3)**

Jonah was extremely angry. In fact, he was so angry he asked God to take his life. We can imagine Jonah saying, "I don't ever want to go back to Israel again. I can't face those people. They will say I am undependable and therefore immoral. You said You would destroy them, but You didn't. I would be better off dead."

For less culpable reasons, the prophet Elijah had said much the same thing: "It is enough!

Now, Lord, take my life, for I am no better than my fathers"(1 Kings 19:4). But the Lord sent to Elijah an angel and prepared a nice little lunch for him when he woke from his exhaustive sleep. He encouraged the prophet, fed him, and put him back to sleep again (verses 5-6).

Jonah's case was very different, however. He was openly attacking God's character. Still, this was an improvement over what we saw in Jonah 1, where Jonah did not talk to God at all but just took off. This was a step upward, for at least now he talked to God about this situation.

Then the Lord said, "Is it right for you to be angry?" (Jonah 4:4)

God could have said, "Since you asked for it, you're done. Drop dead! You didn't learn what you should have in the great fish. I've had it with you. You have completely flopped as a prophet. You are the worst missionary in world history." Instead, we see God very patiently drawing attention to the fact that Jonah's anger was utterly unjustified.

By the way, God's miraculous work at Nineveh in spite of Jonah's mind-set is final proof that even the motivation and attitude of a missionary is not ultimately important. Granted, that is a dangerous statement if taken out of context. But in his letter to the Philippians, Paul said that even if people preached the true gospel (not a Galatian compromise message) out of bad motives such as jealousy, self-interest, or the desire to harm Paul's reputation in Rome, he would rejoice. Whether their attitude was bad or good, whether they loved Paul or not, at least the gospel was being preached!

> Only that in every way, whether in pretense or in truth, Christ is preached; and in this I rejoice, yes, and will rejoice. (Philippians 1:18)

God's Word is what transforms people, not the warmth of personality, eloquence, or friendliness of the preacher. God commands that we preach the truth in love (Ephesians 4:15), but the message is so powerful that it will even get through an unworthy preacher with inadequate motives. The book of Jonah proves it. The people of Nineveh repented just as completely as if Jonah had preached the message in love. Thank the Lord that His Word is powerful enough to overcome the weaknesses of His messengers.

> *So Jonah went out of the city and sat on the east side of the city. There he made himself a shelter and sat under it in the shade, till he might see what would become of the city.* **(Jonah 4:5)**

In other words, Jonah was saying, "Lord, I have now informed You of the real situation: You have made a serious mistake. Whenever You repent, I'll be happy again. I'm going to wait and watch for You to change your mind and destroy the city."

We can be thankful our destiny is in the hands of God and not people like Jonah! Jonah would take one look at some of us and say, "Drop dead." But thank God for Philippians 1:6: "He who has begun a good work in you will complete it until the day of Jesus Christ." His work in us does not continue just until He finds out how sinful we are. Our God, with infinite love, sent His Son into the world so that "whoever believes in Him"—simply believes—"should not perish but have everlasting life" (John 3:16). We have a God who is infinitely different from what Jonah wished Him to be.

> *And the Lord God prepared a plant and made it come up over Jonah, that it might be shade for his head to deliver him from his misery. So Jonah was very grateful for the plant.* **(Jonah 4:6)**

God shows us the ultimate selfishness of Jonah by supernaturally giving him shade from the burning heat of the sun. For this, Jonah was grateful, but it was a gratitude born of selfishness: "I want what I want, my way, for my reputation, in the light of my priorities and my perspective. Now at last You have given me what I deserve: comfort." Some have suggested that because of the permanent damage to his skin from the gastric juices inside the fish, Jonah was highly sensitive to sunshine, and thus he greatly welcomed the relief from the horrible heat.

> *But as morning dawned the next day God prepared a worm, and it so damaged the plant that it withered. And it happened, when the sun arose, that God prepared a vehement east wind; and the sun beat on Jonah's head, so that he grew faint. Then he wished death for himself, and said, "It is better for me to die than to live."* **(Jonah 4:7-8)**

The relief Jonah enjoyed was quickly taken away from him. The plant died and a fierce, burning wind pummeled him, and the heat of the sun again oppressed him. It is interesting that God "prepared," or appointed, a great fish (Jonah 1:17), a plant that grew in one day (4:6), a worm that destroyed the plant (4:7), and then a scorching east wind (4:8). These miracles bring the book back almost to where it began, with a vehement wind blasting Jonah, just as the great wind had blasted the ship. The book of Jonah is beautifully designed. In chapter 1 we saw a great crisis, then prayer, then deliverance, and then vows from the sailors. Chapter 2 also had a great crisis with prayer, deliverance, and vows from Jonah.

God was working on this man and showed him some of the greatest miracles in the history of the world. There are ten of them: The oceanic storm, the casting of the lots, the sudden calming of the sea, the great fish, a three-day trip in the fish, the vomiting out on the shore, the plant, the worm, the fierce burning wind, and—one more!

The greatest miracle of all is found in this last chapter of the book of Jonah, as God miraculously brought His servant into submission. The book does not say that Jonah repented and honored the Lord. But who wrote the story detailing Jonah's anger and his bad attitude? Jonah did! This was his way of saying to his readers, "I did this. I sinned. I am guilty. God wins, and I lose."

Miracle after miracle was accomplished by the preincarnate Christ, who was working on this man Jonah to use him, to teach him, and to change him.

However, the withering of the plant that shaded Jonah and his growing discomfort angered him. Again, he declared that death would be better than enduring this.

> *Then God said to Jonah, "Is it right for you to be angry about the plant?" And he said, "It is right for me to be angry, even to death!"* (Jonah 4:9)

The dialogue here is amazing, as Jonah insisted he was justified in being angry about God's destroying the plant that had provided shade. Yet the One who destroyed the plant had every right to do so, for He was the One who had graciously given it.

> *But the Lord said, "You have had pity on the plant for which you have not labored, nor made it grow, which came up in a night and perished in a night. And should I not pity Nineveh, that great city, in which are more than one hundred and twenty thousand persons who cannot discern between their right hand and their*

*left—and much livestock?" (Jonah
4:10-11)*

Jonah had pity on the plant, which was freely
given to him and required nothing of him. Yet
he did not share God's compassion for the thousands of people in Nineveh. There is more than a
touch of irony in the Lord's final words to the
prophet. In essence, He was saying, "Jonah, even
if you don't care for these people who are deeply
depraved, don't you at least care about the animals? After all, oxen certainly are superior to
shrubs."

What more needed to be said? The Lord
Jesus put this touch on the book: "The men of
Nineveh … repented at the preaching of Jonah;
and indeed a greater than Jonah is here" (Luke
11:32). Our Lord not only can pronounce judgment on people as Jonah did; He can do something Jonah could not: He can save people.
Those who come to Him in faith receive eternal
life provided by His own precious blood on the
cross.

> "But that you may know that the Son
> of Man has power on earth to forgive
> sins"—[Jesus] said to the paralytic, "I
> say to you, arise, take up your bed,
> and go to your house." (Mark 2:10-11)

The healing of the paralytic in Mark 2 was a visual aid. It pointed to something far greater that God's Son was on earth to do: give people everlasting life.

Jesus said, "A greater than Jonah is here." Our beloved Lord Jesus is the eternal second Person of the triune Godhead, by whom the universe was made and before whom all of us someday must appear to give an account of everything that has been entrusted to us. He is the final Judge of all men. He is the coming King of Kings and Lord of Lords. He is the one who could say while hanging on the cross, "Father, forgive them, for they do not know what they do" (Luke 23:34). Truly, One "greater than Jonah is here"!

Jonah wanted to see the wicked Assyrians destroyed. The Lord Jesus wants to save people, and it is due to that fact alone that we are spared the destiny we deserve. If our sinful nature and its potential under the influence of Satan could be seen for what it really is, as God almighty sees it, we would agree with Jeremiah: "The heart is deceitful above all things, and desperately wicked; who can know it?" (Jeremiah 17:9). We deserve vastly worse than anything God has ever done in the way of temporal, visible judgment in the world. But we can say, "Thank You,

God, that You did not conform to Jonah's theology." Otherwise, we would be without hope forever. Thank God that our Lord Jesus Christ is infinitely greater than Jonah.

***

Father, we thank You for this book. May it be etched deeply in our consciences, hearts, and souls that we might be thrilled because You are such a gracious and compassionate God, slow to anger and abundant in loving-kindness, and one who relents concerning calamity.

Lord, You have spared us simply because we believe in your Son. You have prepared us for things "eye has not seen, nor have ear heard, nor have entered into the heart of man" (1 Corinthians 2:9). You have revealed this to us through Your Word and by Your Spirit. May these truths continue with us. May our lives and ministries and testimonies reflect the message You intended for us through this great book. We thank You, and we pray in Jesus' great and glorious name. Amen.

SCRIPTURE INDEX

Jonah: God's Discipline and Love

OTHER RESOURCES

from
Whitcomb Ministries

BOOKS

Christ Our Savior: The Greatest Prophecy—Isaiah 53
The Genesis Flood
Daniel

EXPOSITIONAL BIBLE STUDIES (AUDIO ALBUMS)

Jonah – 6 CDs   Nehemiah – 6 CDs
Daniel – 10 CDs   Malachi – 10 CDs
Esther – 3 CDs

TOPICAL BIBLE STUDIES (AUDIO ALBUMS)

The Five Worlds – 6 CDs
Dinosaurs and Men – 3 CDs
The Bible and Science I – 12 CDs
The Bible and Science II – 6 CDs

CHRISTIAN WORKMAN THEOLOGY COURSES

Jonah – 6 hours DVD   Daniel – 16 hours DVD
Job 18 hours DVD   Ezekiel – 27 hours DVD

For a complete listing of materials, visit our website:
Whitcombministries.org
***

WHITCOMB MINISTRIES

10203 Coral Reef Way, Indianapolis, IN 46256
317-250-5469

Email: Whitcombministry@gmail.com
Listen to archived sermons:
www.sermonaudio.com/whitcomb
http://windowforwomen.blogspot.com

20819288R00084